# *SHROPSHIRE*

Edited by Dave Thomas

First published in Great Britain in 1999 by
*POETRY NOW YOUNG WRITERS*
Remus House,
Coltsfoot Drive,
Woodston,
Peterborough, PE2 9JX
Telephone (01733) 890066



HB ISBN 0 75430 411 6
SB ISBN 0 75430 412 4

# *FOREWORD*

This year, the Poetry Now Young Writers' Kaleidoscope competition proudly presents the best poetic contributions from over 32,000 up-and-coming writers nationwide.

Successful in continuing our aim of promoting writing and creativity in children, each regional anthology displays the inventive and original writing talents of 11-18 year old poets. Imaginative, thoughtful, often humorous, *Kaleidoscope Shropshire* provides a captivating insight into the issues and opinions important to today's young generation.

The task of editing inevitably proved challenging, but was nevertheless enjoyable thanks to the quality of entries received. The thought, effort and hard work put into each poem impressed and inspired us all. We hope you are as pleased as we are with the final result and that you continue to enjoy *Kaleidoscope Shropshire* for years to come.

# CONTENTS

Charlton School

# *The Poems*

## THE ROYAL BRITANNIA

On the 21st day of January
the Royal Britannia set sail.
The ship was going to Morocco
everyone on board was pale.

It's the second day of the voyage
the Queen was getting bored.
The crew were unpacking their luggage
and the food was being stored.

The captain was having a swim
in the big white pool.
It was a bright sunny day
so the Queen had to keep cool.

The ship had a leak
but the crew had courage
so they went down to solve it
on the fifth day of the voyage.

It was the last day of the voyage,
the leak was not fixed well.
And the ship was filling up
it went unnoticed - and there wasn't any bell.

The ship was sinking slowly
nothing could be done.
The crew were all drowning
underneath the sun.

The Queen and the passengers all died
by drowning in the sea.
The ship sank to the bottom
of the Mediterranean Sea.

***James Broome (13)***
***Abraham Darby School***

## THE BOAT

I walk down the dock
to watch a golden coloured boat off for its sail.
The sun is low, but the sky
it leaves a silver shadow.
The boat starts to move
I wonder what it will catch today!
I wave goodbye with a smile on my face
to see the boat sail.
I stand and watch
the still blue . . .

***Rebecca Austin (11)***
***Abraham Darby School***

## FOOTBALL

Football is good
Football is great
When I score a goal I celebrate.
When I'm young I play in the park
When I'm older I'll play in St James's Park.
Soon the trophies will be pouring in
Cabinets bursting at the seams.
Man of the match in every game
England International
World Cup . . . on the way!

***Christopher Horton (11)***
***Abraham Darby School***

# Love

Love is a wonderful thing
which often happens in spring.
You see people kissing
by the bus they were missing.
As always, you hear the birds sing.

Love is a wonderful sight
you see it day or night,
one after another
you see a longing lover
and feel sorry for the poor might.

Love is a terrible thing
when you're waiting for that person to ring.
You wait all night
but still no sight
and then realise they'll never ring.

Love is the saddest thing,
when after all that, they didn't ring.
You feel really mad
but as well you feel sad,
when you tell them
*you'll see them next spring!*

***Ashlie Carter (13)***
***Abraham Darby School***

## SCIENCE

You have lots of studies in science,
biology
and chemistry too.
If you put your mind to it
science isn't really bad
but maths is!
Maths is count, count, count,
equation,
regions,
co-ordinates too.
There are lots and lots of subjects,
English
humanities
drama too!

***Melissa Newton (11)***
***Abraham Darby School***

## CHOCOLATE

*C*ool, smooth and delicious tastes.
*H*orrible! I don't think!
*O*h, how much I like the taste!
*C*an I *ever* give it up?
*O*h, I don't think so
*L*ike it? Oh very much!
*A*t last I've found the meaning of life
*T*he delicious taste of chocolate is so irresistible
*E*at it!
I recommend it . . . !

***Tom Carlon (11)***
***Abraham Darby School***

## THE OWL

The owl has eyes that glow like the sun.
Above all the chaos he rests peacefully.
He longs for the dark
When the hunting can begin.

The owl sits high in his tree.
Glaring at its prey.
He moves not a muscle,
As the mouse scuttles along.

The owl swoops to attack the prey
In its claws the mouse is laid.
Back to his branch the owl flies
He gulps down his dinner and starts again.

***Charlotte Denny (13)***
***Abraham Darby School***

## DAISY - MY DOG

Daisy the dog - is my dog
and I love her so much I could die.
I stroke her and pet her and cuddle her
so much that I make her cry.
You'd think she would resent me
because of me making her cry.
But she doesn't because she loves
me, myself and I . . .
You know now what I give her
doggy treats - too much.
Oh, by the way my dog is the best dog
if you saw her you would love to
*touch . . . !*

***Elisha Taylor (11)***
***Abraham Darby School***

## Morning Sun

The morning sun, morning sun
warm and loving to everyone.
Starts off a warm and friendly day
you'll wish it'll never go away.

The morning sun, morning sun
a fresh start has just begun.
Birds are singing a cheerful song
you'll wish it would last all day long.

The morning sun, morning sun
joy and happiness - so much fun.
The wet gleaming grass the crystal blue sky
I wish I could keep it, I'd like to try.

Goodbye sun, goodbye sun
there's nothing left to be done.
But still inside I will hold
my everlasting heart of gold.

***Kirsty Sands (11)***
***Abraham Darby School***

## Mrs Jones' Bad Day

*M*iss is always shouting,
*R*owing and getting annoyed.
*S*ome people don't like teachers.

*J*ogging or running is better.
*O*ther people are shouting as well.
*N*ever let them beat you
*E*very time try hard
*S*o beat the teachers.

***Ryan Forster (11)***
***Abraham Darby School***

## THE ORPHAN CHILD

T he orphan child
H elp him please
E veryone just passes him in the street.

O nly he can feel that pain
R eally no one else can feel it
P oorly when no doctors are around
H aving a bad time
A ny money to spare
N othing's going fine.

C an anybody help me? he cries
H elp is all I need!
I just want someone to talk to
L ove and a little happiness
D oes anybody care?

***Reuben Griffiths (12)***
***Abraham Darby School***

## THE LIGHTNING STRIKES

The lightning cracks the egg open
the yolk is like the rain.
The thunder is like hooves crashing
the lightning strikes again.
You see it for a second
It's gone . . .
The rain is like a watering can
spilling from the sky.
The rain stops
There's silence . . . !

***Jody Millward (12)***
***Abraham Darby School***

## THEN AND NOW . . .

Look at the world today
Children allowed to run and play
But did you think of little Laurna
What might be lurking around the corner.
Everywhere we look is either murder or violence,
First a laugh . . . but then comes silence.

And what about the flower?
Do you just want the power?
Or do you really care!
Of what becomes of there
Everyone is just so mean,
They don't care for anything green.

But what about 100 years ago?
They didn't care for having a logo!
They didn't throw litter on the floor
They would be more worried if their clothes tore!

So look at what we have today,
A lot of space where everyone would love to play.
But can't because of the pollution
This surely isn't the solution!

All you have to do is put your rubbish in the bin,
Don't commit the sin
Of polluting our mother earth
Don't treat her like some old turf.
So come clean - don't be mean . . . !

***Robyn Elise Haycock (12)***
***Abraham Darby School***

## YOU'LL NEVER WALK ALONE . . .

Liverpool are - as some might say . . .
the strongest team in the UK.
Fowler's nose, and Berger's hair
Redknapp's injury his despair.
Kvarme, Bjornebye and Leo
make up the Norwegion trio.
In the Premiership - Murphy's new
he played in Division One for Crewe.
In the first game Ruddock tumbled
broke his leg but never grumbled.
Owen's young and very cool,
saving games for Liverpool.
From Inter Milan, Paul Ince came
he also played for Man United (shame!)
Midfielders are in good supply
but Carragher is standing by.
Babb and Jones work like a shield
Reidle scores well at Anfield.
Skilful bloke with frizzy hair
Macca's well-loved everywhere.
In defence is McAteer,
he likes bringing up the rear.
Then there's Wright who's never wrong
with Harkness the defence is strong.
David James is six foot tall
that is why he's good in goal.
Roy Evans will never rest
to make the reds the very best.
They try so hard away and at home
with them you know
*you'll never walk alone . . .*

***Rebecca Wade (11)***
***Abraham Darby School***

## Guinea Pigs

I have got two guinea pigs
One's named *Fluffy*
And one's named *Scruffy*.

One's brown and white
The other's a blackish grey.
I have got some guinea pigs
Hip! Hip! Hooray . . .

I bath my guinea pigs
Although they aren't dirty
They try to jump out of the sink
And when they do they wink.

They are really greedy
Eat whatever they can.
If they had to
They would eat a frying pan!

***Natasha Beddoes (11)***
***Abraham Darby School***

## Football

I play football all day long
Kicking, passing, trying to be strong.
It is like a dream come true.
Shooting, passing, heading too!
All my mates will want to play
But I play every day.
I practice and practice until I'm ace
One day I'll be at a bigger place.
Playing for anyone, I don't care
Football will be with me . . . anywhere!

***Daniel Bithell (12)***
***Abraham Darby School***

## Secrets

Can you keep a secret?
Shh . . . Shh . . .!
Have you got a secret?
Shh . . . Shh . . . !
I know you have?
We've all got something to tell
But keep it locked up inside
Shh . . . Shh . . . !
You think no one will understand
Some people will!
Shh . . . Shh . . .!
Yet some people won't!
Shh . . . Shh . . .!
You don't know who will and who won't!
So keep it locked up inside!
Shh . . . Shh . . . !
*And you won't get hurt!*
*Shh . . . Shh . . . !*

***Karlie Allen (11)***
***Abraham Darby School***

## Smell, Hear, See, Feel And Taste

I like the smell of daffodils
I like to hear chattering birds.
I like to see the shining sun.
I like to feel furry dogs.
I like to taste melted chocolate in my mouth.
*Those are a few of my favourite things . . .*

***Sean Mountford (11)***
***Abraham Darby School***

## Darkness And Light

There is a dark cave over there
where it is gloomy and wet.
It is dark and quiet where the cave stands
I walk towards it and take a step
then another
and another
until I walk into the entrance.
I carry on then, all I can see is the
*dark!*
I carry on frightened, the darkness creeps behind me
I trip and fall to the ground.
I get up, wanting to go back
but I wanted to see what was at the end.
Then all of a sudden
I emerge from the dark and gloomy cave into
*light - wonderful light!*
I'm cheerful and happy now I have freedom.
I sit beside a tree the sun shining on
the beautiful green grass.
Then I remembered the dark -
*which really did scare me!*

***Stewart Holmes (13)***
***Abraham Darby School***

## Girls

Girls are so mean and cruel.
I know they're worse than boys
They reckon they know it all!
So I leave it all to them
*Soon they'll find out . . . they don't know it all!*

***Ben Peacock (11)***
***Abraham Darby School***

## My Cat

Thomas is a lazy cat
He is a very good looker.
He ruined his looks one day
When he walked across the cooker.

My brother was making his cereal,
The cat could smell the milk
He sat on the cooker
His tail turned from silk.

The tail turned to crisp
After he sat on the cooker.
(The very good looker)
His tail turned to ginger.

He gave a great big screech,
We wondered what it was.
My brother never got his cereal
The cat had eaten it all!

***Laura Parker (11)***
***Abraham Darby School***

## Fame

I wish I had a pen
to write upon this page.
So I could write some words
to help me earn a wage.
The words they needn't rhyme
or even sound the same
as long as they're neatly written,
they might one day bring me *fame!*

***Kieran MacDonald (11)***
***Abraham Darby School***

## ARE YOU YO-YO MAD!

Are you yo-yo mad?
Are you yo-yo mad?
You're yo-yo mad!

Yo-yo's here
Yo-yo's there.
You just can't help it
Even when they're in the air.

Lots of tricks you can do
Spin them on the floor
Cat's cradle
Even I can do them.

So everywhere you go
You will see them yo-yo's.
So lets face it
They're everywhere . . .

***Michelle Thompson***
***Abraham Darby School***

## MY MAD PETS

Skippity, hoppity, frolic
My dog is an alcoholic.
We all run in fear
When he drinks lots of beer
Skippity, hoppity, frolic.

Skippity, hoppity, filler,
My cat is a serial killer
We all scream and shout
When he gets the axe out.
Skippity, hoppity, filler.

Skippity, hoppity, feeler
My mouse is a drug dealer.
We lock all the doors
When he has drugs on his paws
Skippity, hoppity, feeler.

Skippity, hoppity, funner
My fish is a hit and runner.
We never go far
When he's out in the car
Skippity, hoppity, funner.

***Sophie Webster (12)***
***Abraham Darby School***

## BLACK AND WHITE

Black and white
two colours that go together.
Used in fashion and art
humans that are black and white
seemed to stay apart.

White are superior
colleges and schools.
Own everything nice.
Black has the vile
they're at the bottom of the pile.

A black girl is scared and alone
just because of her colour.
Why should they vilify me
they saw the outside
*not my personality . . . !*

***Catriona Sutherland (13)***
***Abraham Darby School***

## SHOPPING

Going shopping
seeing all the little children
running towards the sweets,
with their faces rosy red.

All the Moms gathering food
putting it neatly into their trolleys.
While the Dads, who are *little kids at heart*
look at the toy cars and guns.

They play with them
you ask them what they are doing
they simply say
'I'm just testing it!'

Then you notice all the shelves
packed with food and goodies.
All labelled by make,
all produced for companies.

Then you look around
and you notice many people are unhappy
except of course the little kids.
And *the kids at heart!*

You realise we humans
are just like the food and goodies.
We are all labelled
by race, sex and age.

*Why . . . !*

***Rebecca Morris (13)***
***Abraham Darby School***

## Zoe's Ballad

Zoe of nine
hasn't been seen for sometime.
Gone without a trace
the police have looked in every place.

Stolen out of her bed
clothes bloodstained red.
Her mother did plea
almost helplessly.

The days wore on
but Zoe was gone.
Her mother's in tears
thinking her worst fears.

An emotional appeal
but was it for real?
The police have their doubts
the truth has to come out.

Nobody have they found
even though they searched all around.
Her mother's not sleeping
for she's always weeping.

Was it a con?
All we know is Zoe's gone.
Someone out there knows
but dare not disclose.

Do her parents hide
the truth inside.
The truth has to be known
for Zoe is still not home . . .

***Amy Laycock (13)***
***Abraham Darby School***

## There Is A Monster

There is a monster who lives in my head.
He's green and slimy and loves to be fed.
His favourite foods are teachers and jelly
Sometimes he likes the occasional welly.
He dances in my bedroom at the darkest time of night.
He peeps behind the curtain and gives passers-by a fright.
He lurks in the shadows
We play hide and seek
He goes to bed inside my head
And I fall fast asleep.

***Katie Graham (11)***
***Abraham Darby School***

## Grandad!

Now when I visit Grandad
it isn't quite the same.
I can't hear him laugh
or joke or say.
'Can I have a cuppa, mate!'
I can't watch him read
his books, or do the football scores.
I can't hear him say
'Hello!' any more.
Now when I visit Grandad
I kneel down and say 'Hello!'
and place some flowers on his grave
hoping that he knows . . .

***Gemma Meller (12)***
***Abraham Darby School***

## The Ghost At Number 10

In the attic at number ten
lives a ghost called giant hen.
He roams the landing at midnight
and gives the children such a fright.
They all scream 'I want my daddy!'
Then they all go in a paddy
which makes the ghost flee.
But then he returns
as a giant bee
and stings them all.
Then at number ten
all you can hear
*is a pin fall . . . !*

***James Ridgway (11)***
***Abraham Darby School***

## English

English is fun
And English is ace
Even better than outer space.
Of all the lessons that I like
English is fun
English is ace . . .

***Chris Docker (12)***
***Abraham Darby School***

## GHOST HOUSE

Every dark and creepy night
there is a house that gives me a fright.
To live next door you have to be brave
to live with spirits, awakened from their grave.
They would rattle their chains, all of the time
and some of them even dripped slime.
They creep around without a sound
and I don't even think they touch the ground.
They claim their victims once a year
not touching them, just killing by fear.
They watch the children on Hallowe'en
knowing they will die with a silent scream.
They open the door with a hollow creak
hoping the children will come to peek.
As they walk through the door to enter the house
there isn't a sound, not even a mouse.
The spirits are waiting
to start the attack
with screams and lights flashing
they come from the back.
The children are startled
they try to run
the stairs are slipping
have the spooks got a gun?
Stuck in a corner
the children let out a shrill.
The ghosts are closing in
it's time for the kill!

***Richard Oliver (13)***
***Abraham Darby School***

## Water And War

I think water cycles
are like the war.
I start off in the sky - floating
the aeroplanes are gliding around.
Suddenly my cloud goes black
the sky is filled with smoke.
I'm being forced out of my space.
There's no room for the aeroplanes anymore.
Suddenly I was hit,
the plane was shot.
I was thundering down to earth
The plane was hurtling to the ground.
*Crash!* I hit the ground, water everywhere.
The plane exploded, fire everywhere,
the sun comes out I'm rising back into the sky
A new plane is being sent up.
I'm rising, joining my friends in the clouds,
the new plane has joined some more planes.
I'm back with my friends,
The plane's with his.
Everything back to normal.
I'm in the sky, floating,
The aeroplane's gliding
and the cycle starts again!

***Natalie Ashman (13)***
***Abraham Darby School***

## A Letter She Wrote Upon Her Death

*My dearest granddaughter*
By the time you read this I shall be gone.
But for my sake, take heed of what I say,
and remember all I told you and I taught you.
With my fondest love to you . . .

I used to be like you
young, and without a care in the world.
Free from the chains of growing old,
never worrying about my life ahead.

My looks were as pretty as yours
as fresh as the clear mornings.
My hair so light I thought it would fly away,
and my eyes, they showed my joy!

My body was young and so full of life,
people would smile at my passing.
I would run, and laugh and skip
people smiled at my young charms

But then old age came and changed me
to the haggard old woman I now am.
Old and just a nuisance and bother
to everyone that knew me.

The hairdresser made my hair
a tangled mess, like a sparrow's nest.
It didn't matter to me though
not since it had become so ashen-grey!

People said that my eyes had lost their sparkle
and that my spring had lost its bounce.
Little children thought I was a grouch
but really I was just sad!

So my granddaughter, read these words
and use them as a warning.
That youth won't last long, so enjoy it
because you won't enjoy old age!

*From your loving grandmother.*

***Ruth Stringer (13)***
***Charlton School***

## ETERNITY

To die for is to live for.
To live for is to learn.
And to learn for you have wisdom
Knocking at your door.

But when it comes to dying
You have to disappear.
No one knows you've gone away
Gone away from here.

So when you're living and learning
Take lots and lots of notes.
'Cos you may end up, up there
Or down in the murky mists of hell.

But most of them are lucky,
Lucky to end up, up there.
To live in peace and harmony,
For the rest of all eternity.
To live in peace and harmony,
For many . . . many years!

***Amy Animashaun (14)***
***Charlton School***

## GRANDPARENTS

'Now dear, are you sure you've got enough?'
Is the frequent saying whenever
I go round to my grandparents for tea.
Gran piles potatoes on my plate
when she only has one pea!

Always giving me newspaper clippings
for one reason or another.
Handing out biscuits
making conversations
about this, that or the other.

The TV's always turned up loud
because without his hearing aids on
Grandpa never hears a sound.
I don't see the point of hearing aids
unless you switch them on.

When I go into another room,
they fret and think I've gone!
But I can't help wondering about
when the tables will be turned,
oh such a sorrowful day.
*And I'll be the one that's fretting*
*When they both go away . . . !*

***Abigail Hulme (14)***
***Charlton School***

## SHIP IN A BOTTLE

I wish I were on the fine blue sea,
With a real sky up above me.
I'd sail by day and I'd sail by night,
And watch the seagulls pass in flight.
But sitting here in this glass bottle,
One day I'm bound to topple,
Into a greasy, waxy sea,
With a painted sky up above me.
Seagulls dangle down from strings,
They just don't move their long white wings,
I wonder why they will not fly,
I wonder why I've no real sky,
Just a ship . . . in a bottle!

***Karl Millsom (10)***
***Charlton School***

## MY REPLY

The crabby old woman in bed number three
never did I think you were once just like me.
Happy and pretty and so full of life
while the elders behind me were ridden with strife.
Every one knew and every one saw
that you weren't the woman that we knew before.
We know the hospital's not a happy place.
we know that we may not agree with your pace.
But please forgive the fact that we never saw
that you weren't the woman - you felt like before!

***Natalie Barton (13)***
***Charlton School***

## My Grandfather's Clock

Tick, tock, tick
the pendulum swings.
Time is running out
while the bluebird sings.

Cracked and broken is its face
it stands right still.
Hands frozen like ice
like a murderer - ready to kill.

My grandfather loves it
he adores his grandfather clock.
But all the children around him
my grandfather they do mock!

For my grandfather is slow
he is tired, weak and old.
And now his clock doesn't work anymore
and it's all covered in mould!

***Richard Thwaites (13)***
***Charlton School***

## Dolphins

Dolphins, dolphins, live in the sea.
Dolphins, dolphins, a friend for you and me.
Watch them swimming and crashing through the waves,
Go deep under - in and out the caves,
They follow the boats that are in the sea,
As they dive down under - to get their tea.
Fishes, fishes everywhere, they swim about without a care.
Dolphins, dolphins, live in the sea,
Dolphins, dolphins a friend for you and me.

***Elaine Hayward (12)***
***Charlton School***

## If Only Houses Could Talk

Jobs a plenty for nature's busy-bodies.
Life in the garden buzzing and blooming.
The oozing, squelching, sweet honey
Drips tantalisingly close to the tip of your tongue.
The smell oozes and wafts upon the kitchen's finery.
The smell presses on
Up the screeching, squeaking, staircase.
The walls are cluttered with beastly weapons,
Fresh with memories of bloody battles of past.

The house a majestic war-horse
Looks tired - it feels tired.
Its character aches to come out.
Sixteenth century slate black beams
Adds to the effect.
The rooms presence towers over you
Your jaw aches in amazement
At the Colossus . . . before you!

***Tom Carver (13)***
***Charlton School***

## Dolphins

Sleek, graceful dolphins
Elegantly sliding through the water
Faster than any car or boat.
Lively creatures glimmering in the sun,
More beautiful than a model
More glimmering than an actress
Their natural beauty's more friendly than men
Glimmering, glittering, they're my *friends.*

***Kirsty Louise Oldroyd (11)***
***Charlton School***

## I Hate The Park

I hate the park - especially in the dark!
When the night goes cold I shiver from head to toe
Then after that I'm lost! I don't know where to go.
No one is around, I'm starting to get scared.
Should I ask someone where to go or will they
Just not care?
The swings start swinging, I hear an echoing noise.
A gust of wind blows, rubbish blows everywhere.
I start to yell
I want the company of my toys.
Around the corner someone - *I'm saved!*
It's my mum . . .

***Kerry Hutching (12)***
***Charlton School***

## When We Went To Apley Wood

When me and my friends went to Apley Wood
It was brill
It was good
We saw trees that were big and tall.
We saw plants that were tiny and small.
We found leaves that were yellow and green.
Me and my friends went on the rope swing.
They fell off and had a sting
As we walked down the path
There was a great giraffe.
Then we ran out of the wood
*As fast as we could . . . !*

***Tom Stone (12)***
***Charlton School***

## TV

The inventor of TV was a wonderful guy.
Now we can all sit watching Sky!
Every day we're glued to the set
Whether outside it's dry or wet.
On comes Coronation Street
And the adults rush for a seat.
If the sport comes on, the men get the beer
It might be football or driver's in gear.
Then on comes a movie - so put tiny children to bed.
It could be a horror or comedy instead.
Whatever seems to be on TV
It's always being watched by me . . .

***Anthony Pearce (12)***
***Charlton School***

## FIVE

Five are the best band around,
They have got the coolest sound,
I am their biggest fan,
I'd like to meet them if I can,
To collect their records costs a lot,
You will need a big money pot,
I think Scott is the best,
Sean acts like a real pest,
Abs, Rich and J,
These are all OK,
Boyzone are old and sad,
But Five are new and fab!

***Leanne Meredith (11)***
***Charlton School***

## My Next Door Neighbour

My next door neighbour Charlie
He's about eighty eight
He's really old and grouchy
And that's what I really hate!

My next door neighbour Charlie
His hair is snowy white
People are scared of him
Just in case he'll kick and bite

My next door neighbour Charlie
I'm not scared of him
Because he is very slow
And he's got a bad limb

My next door neighbour Charlie
He's as deaf as a bat
He wears his old clothes
And his scraggy old hat

My next door neighbour Charlie
He walks down the street and sings
And his singing is really, really bad
I can say other things
But that will make him mad.

***Karl Steadman (12)***
***Charlton School***

## The Dog

I walk the dog every day,
So it can play,
We get home for a drink,
In the corner it shall sit,
He goes to bed, its name is Fred
That leads him to a dream,
He has a dream, which seems to be,
Counting sheep 1, 2, 3,
Over the hurdles they must go,
As if they were at a show.

His colour is black and white,
To look at him would give you a fright,
But if you really knew Fred,
You could take him to your bed,
His feet are frightening,
And are good for fighting,
His teeth are sharp and small,
But he could use them in a brawl,
He is strong as a house,
But as quiet as a mouse.

When Fred awakes in the morning dew,
The first thing he does is go to the loo,
Into the garden he does go,
Far and wide, even in the snow,
I call his name,
And he thinks it's a game,
He barks out loud,
Into the house he goes,
Jumping up on my clean clothes.

***Amanda Cross (12)***
***Charlton School***

## BUMBLE BEE

I saw it there yesterday, as pretty as can be,
Sitting on a flower is a little bumble bee,
His black and yellow stripes, gleaming in the sun,
I think this little bumble bee is having lots of fun.

Flying gliding, soaring round and round,
Without his little body even touching the ground.
Night is coming, coming near,
It's now time for him to disappear,
It is now winter but spring is clear,
That it shall be coming soon here.

The honey is ready in the bumble bee's nest,
Now it is time for him to have a rest,
Now he is resting will I ever see,
This little bumble bee,
Will he fly around my garden ever again?
Just see, just wait and see.

***Carla Taylor (12)***
***Charlton School***

## MAZDA

Mazda, Mazda, white and red, come on everybody
Smooth Mazda, loud Mazda, fast Mazda, what a Mazda!
Come on everybody come and help me save for my Mazda
I love Mazdas, come on everybody join in the fun
Black car, blue car, what colour? I don't know
Yellow car, pink car I don't think I'm going to have a blue Mazda
Come on everybody and join the fun, it goes fast, it goes smooth
It is loud, come on everybody I have the car and I'm hitting the road
I'm going to my friend's house and join the fun.

***Craig East (11)***
***Charlton School***

## WINTER WARMTH

Winter is cold, wet and dried up,
Blowing out air, cold, warmth,
Snow falling, everything turned white,
Lost in a world, unusual to the naked eye.
Winter is cold, wet and dried up.

Love sparks up,
Life around you warms up,
Rivers again flow,
Everything red, melting words,
Winter is cold, wet and dried up.

The kettle pops, steam pours out,
Into the cold world around, glowing a purple flame
Pull tight the covers, hide down below, like a cocoon
Until the energy seeps out, lost forever, Winter is cold, wet
*and all dried up!*

***Paul Edwards (14)***
***Charlton School***

## GOING TO A SHOW

My pony gallops as fast as the wind.
He races with another.
I know he could win.
Flying high over the jumping poles,
'Goodness gracious, what a great show!'
He gallops faster and faster, taking over another horse,
He is nearly there, at the finish line at the end of the course.

***Connie Li (11)***
***Charlton School***

## THE EXTRAORDINARY FOOTBALL TEAM

The teams parted
The game started
They asked for much more pay
The managers did not know what to say.

Shocked, surprised, amazed
The crowd just gazed
The team got up
Hoping to win the FA Cup
They ran their little hearts out
Again the crowd started to shout
Then we scored
The crowd stood and roared
The whistle went, end of the game
For the other team, misery and shame.

***Casey Starling (12)***
***Charlton School***

## AUTUMN POEM

As I walk through bare trees of brown
their leaves lying scattered along the ground
all crisp and dry, a golden tone, they crunch and crack as I walk home.
Frost-bitten fingers, cold wisps of wind, fine lighthouses with
warmth within.
Wrapped up children all warm and pale, blue lips quivering in
strong autumn gales.
Frosty morning with sunlit skies, a cosy feeling sitting inside.
Crackling fires with evening dawning, little children begin yawning.
Night arrives, we all sit down feeling warmth all around.
We go to bed and close our eyes, another autumn day is yet to arrive.

***Vikki Hedges (12)***
***Charlton School***

## I Really Miss My Mom

I can't believe it.
She's really dead.
My mom.
Now I feel like there's nothing to live for.
She was always there for me.
I always told her I loved her.
'Bye Mom' I said, as I leaned over her
and damped her with my tears.
Somehow I feel as if she's still with me.
Sometimes I think I can hear her voice
whispering to me.
But obviously I can't.
I really miss my mom.
But there's nothing I can do about it.

***Rachel Wilbrey (12)***
***Charlton School***

## Friends

Friends are helpful
Some friends are terrible
but if you have a friend
like Johanna you're sure
to have fun.

Johanna is a perfect friend.
I think I will like her till life's end.
If anything should happen to Johanna
I will always be there forever and ever.

***Rachel Binnersley (11)***
***Charlton School***

## Love!

Love is a most
Splendid thing.

Love is great!
But sometimes bad.

Love can be heartbreaking,
But sometimes fun.

Love is a gift
To make life lift

Love can be depressing
So let your love ripe

Love is the best
gift anyone could give.

***Lyndsey Howells (11)***
***Charlton School***

## Separation

S is for sadness
E is for evil
P is for persuasion
A is for angry
R is for revenge
A is for advice
T is for terrible
I is for incredible
O is for open-hearted
N is for nastiness.

***Tara O'Reilly (11)***
***Charlton School***

## Love

Love can be great!
But can be bad!
It can be depressing
And you could get hurt
But believe in yourself and your
Love will flirt
Love is splendid
But sometimes offended
It can go right
It can go wrong.
Love is a gift
Which will make your love lift.
That is the best day a boy can give.
Love can be heartbreaking.
But most times, fun
Most love endings you'll
End on the run.

***Caroline Holloway (11)***
***Charlton School***

## Natural Thoughts

Tranquil meadows of soft velvet grass,
Roaming hills, reminders of the past.
Shining stars of distant galaxies,
Water falling brings back memories.

Leaves falling off aged trees,
Breeze whistling of heavens above.
Deep intense buzzing of a bumble bee,
The opening of a flower, signalling love.

***Amanda Habberley (13)***
***Charlton School***

## DOWN MEMORY LANE

Down Memory Lane,
The wind whistles,
The leaves rustle,
The crops grow.

Down Memory Lane,
Your granny smiles,
You smell apple pie,
and bacon sizzling.

Down Memory Lane,
You're tying your shoelaces,
You're playing in the snow,
You're running through a field of crops.

Down Memory Lane,
You go for a stroll,
You find a haunted house,
*Aaaaah!*

Down Memory Lane,
I go to school,
I go to church,
I go home.

But that was all a memory
they will never go,
I'm home now.

***Lauren Millward (11)***
***Charlton School***

## THE BIG MATCH!

It's England v France
The World Cup Final
Owen's playing
We must win now
France kick-off
England tackle
And launch an attack
Shearer makes a run
Plays the ball back
Owen has a crack!
*Ooh!* It just goes wide
France on the attack
It's Thierry Henry,
He shoots from 30 yards!
Comfortable save for Seaman
This is end to end stuff.
Seaman boots it up
Owen on the volley!
What a . . . *goal!*
England 1-0 up
This is amazing!
Half-time whistle goes
England take the kick-off,
Shearer passes to Beckham
He takes a shot!
It's gone in!
2-0 to England!
5 minutes left
England score again!
Andy Cole, 3-0, full-time.

***David Barnett (12)***
***Charlton School***

## Haunted House

Dare you step in?
Dare you open the door?
Creak, creak!

You can hear something inside
You step in,
Creak, creak!

You're inside now,
The door slams, oh no!
Creak, creak!

You look at the door,
Something touches your back,
Creak, creak!

Turn around,
What's that?
Creak, creak!

The eyes are moving in the pictures
They're watching you,
Creak, creak!

Run towards the door
You're locked in
*Agghh!*

***Joanna Biffin (11)***
***Charlton School***

## SHOES

I have
Flippers,
Slippers,
Flat shoes,
Tap shoes,
Ballet shoes,
Rap shoes,
Hiking shoes,
Biking shoes,
Special shoes,
Play shoes,
Skating shoes,
Dating shoes,
Training shoes,
Raining shoes,
High shoes,
Tie shoes,
Sand shoes,
Land shoes,
Now you know,
Why I can't decide,
What shoes to wear,
In snow,
In rain,
Or just simply lazing on a chair!

***Hannah Gough (11)***
***Charlton School***

## LATE

I'm late, I'm late
If I don't hurry Mr Spickton
will use me as fish bait.
I hate school
I'll tell you something,
school does not rule.

I've been saved
We've got a supply teacher
called Dave.
I've got to stay in at break
I've got a cake to bake

We were going to watch a video
We didn't though.
It was Baby's Day Out
Something to shout about

It's lunch-time
Food time, soggy chip time
Funeral time.

***Andrew Wright (11)***
***Charlton School***

## THE NEW WORLD

In 1492 Columbus set sail to the west.
Hoping to be successful in his quest.
He was looking for India from his ship,
So far he'd had a really good trip.

One day he was sitting, the sea was calm,
A whale attacked, but doing no harm.
He saw some land and got excited.
All of the crew were really delighted.

They got to shore, jumped off the boat,
Praying it would stay afloat.
Everyone was looking for human life.
Then Chris nearly got in a bit of a strife.

'There's no one here for miles around,
I think we should take this piece of ground.
I'll name it in honour of the King and Queen,
America, the best country we've seen!'

***Jonathan Simpson (13)***
***Charlton School***

## NIGHT

The sky is full of light at night,
The moonlight casts its shadows,
The loud squawk of the owl
And the badger creeping from its hole,
The little squeaking of the bat
As the silent creeping of the cat,
The branches rise and then fall,
I hear the wind and its call,
The moon that is full, cast over by cloud,
The wolf and its howl,
The bumpy ground filled with dew,
The night that feels like new,
The moths flutter in the air,
Not without a care,
The squeaking of a gate,
The cuckoo and its mate,
The early chirping of the birds,
Up in the trees as they twist and curl,
The sky is coloured pink and blue,
Covered in a grey mist it's true.

***Johanna Mann (11)***
***Charlton School***

## STRANDED

I walk alone on sandy plains,
Desolate and cold is my heart.
Things dwell within my waters that man will never see,
Yet I have no companion.
No other like me.
There are some that call me salty,
When they are strictly pure.
They are far from me,
In this lonely world,
In places I am loved,
And others greatly feared,
For both calm and wild am I.
I took explorers far and wide,
And many a man I've slain.
I'm given many names,
But I am all one.
For some I am life, while others play in the sun,
I am a silk, wet with foam.
I am slave to the wind, like man is to me,
They are pennies to a millionaire,
They go one by one, yet more will come,
Sometimes by my strength they are lost,
A guilty soul have I.
I see all and hear all,
And forever more it shall be.

***Sarah Louise Farley (12)***
***Charlton School***

## Chicago Hope

They walked on to the court,
Their heads held high.
Scottie Pippen was not there,
And everyone wondered why.

It turned out injury,
Kept him off the court.
And after 5 minutes,
Jazz were winning, 6 to nought.

Utah Jazz were storming,
Chicago in a trance.
Jordan saw an opening,
And dominated his first chance.

At half-time they were drawing,
Bulls playing their best.
The coach was very pleased,
Heart pounding in his chest.

Jordan was superb,
Longley, what a player.
Harper scoring all the points,
And Rodman controlling his layer.

The end of the game was approaching,
With everyone trying to score.
Everyone held their breath,
When Jordan was pushed to the floor.

Everyone got excited,
Because Bulls had won the game.
Utah Jazz were crying,
*Arghhhhh!* What a shame.

***Craig Robert Webb (12)***
***Charlton School***

## AMERICA

When I first went to Florida,
My eyes were open wide,
I looked inside the candy stores,
And glared at the huge rides.

When I first went to Florida,
I had a great surprise,
I ate beefburgers every day,
And threw up on the rides.

When I  first went to Florida,
The people were so nice,
The people told me I should go,
And see those famous mice.

When I first went to Florida,
It was so very hot,
I drank water all the time,
And one day I even found a dime.

Now it's time to go back home,
I am so very sad,
But now I know I will be back,
And that makes me feel glad.

***Danielle Jarvis  (12)***
***Charlton School***

## ZZZZZZ!

When I go to sleep at night,
I sometimes wake up in a fright.
I shake and turn, but nothing works!
I have to go and iron some shirts.
I go back to my room, in my bed,
But I can't sleep, I count sheep instead.

When I run out of sheep at night.
I change to rabbits, or pigs in flight.
I count and count, but no sleep yet,
Oh no! I find my sheets are wet!
The pigs have landed and now I'm tired,
I'm late in the morning for work
I'm
*Fired!*

***Martin Brady (14)***
***Charlton School***

## Dogs

Dogs, the one who cheers your lonely walk,
The one who makes your life complete.
Dogs, what would we do without them?
Dogs, the one who cheers you when you're sad.
The one who keeps you warm at night.
Dogs, the one who protects you in all that you do.
Dogs, how would life be without them?
Dogs, the way they run and jump,
How they silently touch the ball,
Nose touching it in the air.
The way they walk with you, side by side.
Could we live without them?
Dogs, the one who pines for you when you're away,
Thinking of you every minute of the day.
Dogs, we really need them in our lives.
Just think, the house wouldn't be the same without a dog.
Everything would be so quiet.
Dogs, I daren't think what life would be like without a dog.
Dogs, just think, we would have no one to spend our money on.
I wonder just how much money we do spend on them?
*Dogs*, how could we live without them?

***Sophie Yates (11)***
***Charlton School***

## The Red Dwarf Cat

Cat was walking along the deck,
then he saw Lister who had
broken his neck.
The cat said 'Tish tish'
and went off the get some fish.
Along deck 2, he stopped walking
and said to himself 'How am I looking?'
He pulled out his mirror and said
'I'm looking nice'
and felt like catching some mice.
He went to the food machine
and asked for fish and mice topped off with cream.
Pleased with himself, the cat walked on
and from deck 2, he was soon gone.
Groovily walking to the disco room,
when he came across a big, brown broom.
Cat found it quite amusing
but Rimmer found it quite abusing.
He said to cat that the prickles were lethal,
and the sharp bits were like a needle.
'Oh well' said cat,
I'll have to make do with this hat

***Owen Williams (12)***
***Charlton School***

## MEATBALLS

The thing I like best
Yes, most of all
In my whole life
They're called meatballs.

They're fat and juicy
Nice and warm
With peas, carrots
And sweetcorn.

I eat them for breakfast
I eat them for tea
I eat them whenever
I feel hungry

If ever I'm hungry
And want a meatball
I go to the freezer
And steal them all

I dream about meatballs
I could eat them all day
Mum gets them from Tesco's
And sometimes Safeway.

***Simon Humphreys (12)***
***Charlton School***

## Cats

Cats, a wealthy meal of chicken and lamb,
Cats, licking their lips from side to side,
Cats, sees a bird on the fence,
Cats, prowling through the flap like a cunning fox,
Cats, have to be quiet,
Cats, slowly does it, slowly does it,
Cats, the bird knows he's there, you can see fear,
Cats, through the flap
Cats, jumping over a garden hose,
Cats, his paws stuck in garden debris,
Cats, thoughts racing through his mind,
Cats, will he ever have an extra snack,
Cats, creeping along the garden wall,
Cats, nearly there, nearly there,
Cats, the bird has hopped away,
Cats, the cat hides slyly in a rose bush,
Cats, the birds has a cunning plan,
Cats, he is moving closer,
Cats, the bird is eating nuts,
Cats, the cat is there,
Flap! The bird is free from the cat!

***Sarah Hickey (11)***
***Charlton School***

## Pray To God

Every night I pray
And every night I look up to God
Will he give me answers
Or will he turn away?
I really need a friend
And maybe he's the one
God created me
And now I need his help.

My mind is going mad
God has answered me
My mind is full of questions
To ask the powerful Father
I've found the perfect friend
He's the one for me
And now he's answered my questions
What else shall I ask?

***Natasha Corbett (11)***
***Charlton School***

## Hidden Truths

I look through my window,
The trees hide the truth.
Cars pass my window,
The trees hide the truth.
People pass my window,
The trees hide the truth.

People unsuspecting of
What the trees hide.
People ignorant of
What the trees hide.
People disregarding,
What the trees hide.

The trees hide drink and drugs,
So nobody sees them.
The trees hide shattered lives,
So nobody sees them.
The trees hide the truth,
So nobody sees it.

***Kathryn Davies (15)***
***Charlton School***

## GHOST

Up on the hill
there's a mansion
where nobody goes.
It is known to be haunted
and it is very, very old,
100 years in fact,
maybe older, no one knows.

Screaming, shouting comes from there
dare you to go, *no no!*
No one goes, will you?
In fact I've been down there myself
I'll tell you about it.

The corridors are dark
cobwebs all around.
I heard a noise, I ran,
I shouted, I screamed.
I could not find the way out
I looked and looked.

I sat down
I was scared
I felt sleepy
I did not wake up!

***Claire Milly Finch (11)***
***Charlton School***

## MY FAT CAT

My fat cat is chubby and round,
He sleeps all day then waddles around.
He can't jump high,
'Cos he's eaten the pie.

My fat cat is a big ginger bubble,
If he falls over he's in great big trouble.
When he lies down he can't get back up,
So he whines and whines and we pick
Him up.

***Chris Doody (12)***
***Charlton School***

## CRICKET

England vs Australia
England in first
Chrimes and Atherton to bat
Chrimes at the crease
Warne comes up to bowl
Phew! It's gone wide
Warne bowls again, I hit it. Yes it's a four!
*What a shot!*

End of the over
Phew! 4 runs for 0 wickets
Atherton at the crease
McGrath comes up to bowl, Atherton hits it,
It goes for a single.
Chrimes at the crease
McGrath bowls again. Yes! It's a six
*Superb shot!*

End of the over
It's lunch
Chrimes and Atherton walk off the field,
The crowd cheer them
England, 111 runs for 0 wickets.

***Nathan Chrimes (11)***
***Charlton School***

## FOOTBALL TRAINING

Monday:
Practised kick-ups,
ended up in
a load of mess ups.

Tuesday:
Mastered my crossfield kick, hit my
friend Nick and made him sick.

Wednesday:
Improved my 25 yard shot,
kicked it too far, went through
the door, smashed
my mom's best antique pot.

Thursday:
Practised heading the ball,
hit the brick wall.

Friday:
Practised my tackles and dives,
slipped on my backside, straight
on top of a bee hive.

Saturday:
Should I give football up?
Yes, I know, I'll play tennis.

***Jason Veric (11)***
***Charlton School***

## NINTENDO 64 DREAMIN'

Movement is the key,
The rumble pak vibrates
your whole body,
It's like I am in a world of
my own,
I imagine that I am
Link, Mario or even
Banjo-Kazooie,
I have conquered Mario but
I don't care I'll play it again,
It's in 3-D and it's like reality
you know,
Nintendo best beware
Dreamcast is coming.

***Nicholas Sutton (11)***
***Charlton School***

## LOVE

Love is a passionate feeling deep inside
Love is there and all around you and within you
It's something or someone you feel for
It can be a tingling feeling over your body
Or a deep slushiness running through you
Love can soften your heart or break it
You usually think it will last forever
The colour of love inside you is red
And tastes like hot melted chocolate on a cold day
I think it smells like fruity perfume.

***Libby Edwards (11)***
***Charlton School***

## AUTUMN

Autumn
is fun, there
are conkers and
crispy leaves
falling off the trees
Misty morning and
slippery grass
Lots of different colours
all around. Swaying trees
in the wind
rainy day, cold night
and Hallowe'en and bonfire night
Snow, ice, rain and lots, lots more
I like autumn, it's a lot of fun
and a whole lot more.

***Colin Whitfield (11)***
***Charlton School***

## ICE-CREAM

I is for ice-cream man
C is for Cornetto
E is for eating them

C is for calypso
R is for rocket ice-cream
E is for enjoyment
A is for apple flavoured ice-cream
M is for melting in the sun.

*I love ice-cream.*

***Kerry Sankey (11)***
***Charlton School***

## What Is?

What is that creak upon the stair?
I go and look but there's nothing there.
What is that shadow on the wall?
It can't be me for I'm too small.

What is that noise under my bed?
The very sound fills me with dread.
What is that light in my room
That lights a corner in the gloom.

What is that knock upon my door
Will I be frightened forever more?
What is that knife above my head
What is my life, now I'm dead?

***Michael Hood (11)***
***Charlton School***

## Football

Football, such a skilful game
Especially when the best teams are
Playing,
Like Man United, Liverpool and Arsenal.
When these teams are playing
I don't know who to support.
But when Man United are playing I will
Always be on their side.
Even though Man United lost the
Premiership last year, they will be back
This year with more strength, power and
Skill.

***Mark Barr (11)***
***Charlton School***

## A PINEAPPLE

A big, fat, juicy *pineapple,*
All prickly, like a hedgehog on the outside,
But all soft and juicy on the inside,
It makes your mouth water so much,
That you dribble thinking about it.
You lick your lips and slurp all the
Juice up from around your mouth,
I can smell that lovely fruity smell,
Of a lush *pineapple.*

You get all different sizes, big,
Small, medium and even tinned,
It's juicy, glistening and sparkling in the sun,
How much I want to drink that fruity,
Fruity drink on a hot, hot day.

***Ami Johnson (11)***
***Charlton School***

## CHILDHOOD

How wonderful to be a child
So innocent and carefree
The harsh, dark world you've never known
The pain you just can't see.

It doesn't last long though
For you're so eager to learn more
Time flies and unconsciously
You push childhood out of the door.

***Alison Mayor (15)***
***Charlton School***

## Airport

We arrive at the car stay,
We park our car,
Out come the suitcases.
On the minibus we go, we are off!
Birmingham airport comes nearer and nearer.
The minibus stops, we get off
Dad gets a trolley.
We go to check-in, we put the suitcases on the conveyor belt
And away they go.
We go upstairs to the departure lounge
Our flight gets called, we go to the gate.
We board the Britannia plane
There are lots of other people aboard.
The plane takes off
And away we go.
I am really excited.

***Laura Brierley (11)***
***Charlton School***

## Upon Telford Plaza

Earth has not anything to show more ghastly
Devil would he be of soul who could
A sore sight so ugly in its glorious surroundings
This site now spoiled
The beauty of the morning, now destructed
Never has the sun been hidden from view
Never felt so aggrieved at the monstrous structure
Dear God! Let the people see light of day.

***Simon Davenport (15)***
***Charlton School***

## Mystery

It is a mystery
Every night I see it
I walk through it
It is my own place
My private place
A tunnel winding
A tunnel curving and swerving
It has many doors
But they are all locked
Locked tightly
It is long and tiring
It is beautiful
Trees with gold and silver and diamond leaves
As I near the end I will see a light
A light that glows on the purple walls and the gold floors
At the end, a beautiful sight
A huge lake alive but somehow still
Swans swim by
Mermaids sit on the rock
Playing magical music with harps
I go there every night
But when I get to the lake I always wake up
It is a mystery.

***Rhiannon Adams (11)***
***Charlton School***

## Colourful Moods

When you're in a mood
And know this is not rude,
Don't you just find?
There's only thing on your mind.

Every mood has a colour
Even the colour of the rice called Müller.
Don't just hide it away
Let your mind and your feelings play.

Yellow is the colour
That symbolises happiness.
It also is the colour
That surrounds the lioness.

Red equals anger
That's the mood you feel,
Sometimes you have to kneel
When you're making an appeal.

Black is the colour
Of depressing times
When nothing goes right
And you just don't feel bright.

Pink is for sloppy
When you feel all floppy,
Your heart's just beating
And you know that you're competing.

***Cherida Jones (12)***
***Charlton School***

## FRIDAY

Yes, it's Friday, can't wait to go home!
Two whole days till school again,
Yes, it's Friday, what should I do?
Ice skating? Cinema? Shopping or watch TV?
Yes, it's Friday, we're having pizza for tea,
Tomorrow, a burger and on Sunday, a roast,
Yes, it's Friday, I can stay up late tonight,
I'll stay up till at least ten,
Yes, it's Friday, I'll have a lie-in tomorrow,
I'll stay in bed till twelve,
Yes, it's Friday, I can wear my own clothes,
T-shirts, jeans, whatever I want,
Oh no! It can't be Friday!
That's homework time!

***Hannah Saunders (12)***
***Charlton School***

## NESSIE

She hides at the bottom of the deep loch,
Waiting for people to give them a shock.

The waters are eerie, misty and black,
Keep an eye out behind your back!

She comes to the surface looking rather grim,
You look at her in amazement, then she starts to swim.
You grab you camera but to your surprise,
There is nothing there but a swarm of flies.
You sit there for hours thinking about it,
Tell anyone and they will call you a twit!
You finally go home, half asleep,
Nessie is a secret that you want to keep.

***Jane Fletcher (12)***
***Charlton School***

## Shopping

I go shopping at the weekend,
Buy clothes, see how much I can spend,

I buy lots of sweets, make-up too,
I bought a lovely dress, it is bright blue,

I'll buy a purse though I've got lots more,
I'd buy no more, to my mum I swore.

Now I think it's time for lunch,
Look at those strawberries, munch, munch, munch.

I bought a skirt, a shirt too, now my only problem is
where am I going to wear it to.

Now it is time to go home,
I think next weekend I'll need a loan.

***Rebecca Sharpe (12)***
***Charlton School***

## My Sister

Sister, sister,
You are a little blister,
Why are you always that way?
Why don't you go outside to play?

Sister, sister,
You are a little blister.
You're always hanging about,
Why do you look like a trout?
Why do you make me shout?

***Jessica Millard (11)***
***Charlton School***

## Bank Robber

On cashier I advanced, with a grin on my face,
And a spring in my pace.
I was set dead ahead,
But my brains were in bed.

I slammed down my hand, 'Cash I demand.'
Bell sound,
Dogs hound.

With senses about me, I tried to get out,
I ducked and dived, and darted about.
Zigged and zagged, and darted some more,
In an all-out attempt to reach the door.

All pieces intact, I escaped alive,
On the run, no time to take five.
With police in pursuit,
I was swift in my route.
I ducked and dived and darted about.
Zigged and zagged and darted some more,
In an all-out attempt to gain some floor.

But all to no avail, the police have closed in,
Now it's certain I'll do time for my sin.

So, I've finally been caught, and you know what they say,
Don't do the crime, because crime doesn't pay.

***David Cains (12)***
***Charlton School***

## What's In A Poem?

As I sit here and ponder,
On this poem I read,
My mind starts to wander,
And my brain can't concede.

What use is a verse?
Just words on a page,
Can't heal like a nurse,
Not a colour like beige.

Yet what does it mean,
To put one's feelings down?
To capture a dream,
To record a frown.

These emotions I bear,
All bottled up inside,
In words I can share,
In this paper I confide.

They say that a problem told,
Is a problem halved by two,
So reader, young or old,
My problem's now with you.

***David Hubbleday (16)***
***Charlton School***

## I Never . . .

Every day I saw you
Knew you didn't care
Can't forget the past
Pain too hard to bear

Everybody else knew
How we felt inside
And though we longed to show it
We were beaten by our pride

I never told my secret
And yours, you hid away
Both too proud to show it
Not knowing how to say . . .

It was almost too obvious, but not to us
The feelings that we hid
The masked looks and hidden pain
In everything we did

Now you've gone and I'm alone
I've wished that I would die, 'cos
I never said I loved you
I never said goodbye.

***Becci Howarth (16)***
***Charlton School***

## I'M SORRY

I'm sorry for failing my final exams
and for going to town when I should have been at school.
I'm sorry for smoking in my room at home
and for staying out and not coming back 'til late.
I'm sorry for doing the opposite to everything I was told
and for dying my hair and piercing my nose.
I'm sorry for stealing money from you
and for injecting poison and sniffing glue.
I'm sorry for being with so many different boys
and for my strange music that made so much noise.
I'm sorry for the embarrassment of the police car on the drive
and for all the involvement I had in crime.
I'm sorry for hating everything you did
for all the hurt I caused
and that you had me for a kid.
I'm sorry that you could not see
that all I ever wanted was
for you to notice me.

***Jenna Guppy (15)***
***Charlton School***

## SISTER, SISTER

Sister, sister
Always hanging around
Because you're a blister
Get back on the ground

Sister, sister
Why are you in my hair?
Go away!
I don't care where.

***Emma Elizabeth Dawe (12)***
***Charlton School***

## My Three Minutes

Like the morning rain
The lyrics of a love song
But the melody is a strain
And the harmony sounds wrong

Reminds me of a time
When the baselines were deep
When my head was filled with rhyme
And the days didn't end with sleep

Echoing through my soul
Is the beat of the drum
That made my life whole
And left my senses dumb

Guitar slashes like a knife
Shattering the silence
That once was my life
That consumed my existence

My three minutes of justification
Gave rhythm to the drone
That once was my affection
In the silence I listen alone.

***Richard Palin (15)***
***Charlton School***

## Animal Poem

My cats and dog fight all day,
I wish they didn't, I pray, I pray.
Woof, woof, miaow, miaow,
Stop fighting right now!

***Darrell James Bridgwater (11)***
***Charlton School***

## You Said

You said I was your girl
I was the only one for you
You'd love me with a passion
And a burning that was true

You said the fairest lady
Had nothing next to me
That the stars in all the heavens
Gazed down on my beauty

You said if I ever left you
Your world would crumble down
And if I was ever sad or scared
That you would be my clown

You said you'd always love me
That you'd never leave my side
We'd be together for eternity
You said it, but you lied.

***Esther Clark (15)***
***Charlton School***

## Gym

The coach is the worst
Mark will most probably burst
They all rehearsed
Kyle, Dan and Mark were all cursed

Igor the coach shouts like hell
And Kyle rang the bell
Mark makes the dough
Dan makes a very pretty bow.

***Lee Maddox (11)***
***Charlton School***

## The Bloodstained Tear

The tears of a nation fill rivers of blood
They weep, for they'd turn back the clock, if they could
The power of love binds them tightly together
The loss of their loved ones be with them forever.

Tears and blood, blood and tears
They try but can never forget wasted years
At night they hear their friends' dying screams
And the visions, so terrible, that haunt all their dreams.

Phantom faces at the window, ghostly shadows on the wall
But all the hating fades afar, as the rain begins to fall
This blessing from heaven melts away the pain of all those years
And falls within the river, to mingle with the tears.

Too many lives were wasted, too much blood was shed
I only hope God wept for them, one tear for each one dead
Sometimes in the silence, you can see an Earth reborn
And sometimes in the chaos there's a world that's ripped and torn.

Treasure the courage of the fallen, and those who made it through
Remember what they died for, because they fought for you
The lost souls of the soldiers, who perished in the flame
Will ever be remembered by a little fall of rain.

***Jenny Hazelwood (16)***
***Charlton School***

## The Bee Is Dead!

The bee is dead,
It won't get up,
My brother said 'It's gone to bed,'
It hit me on the head,
That's why the bee is dead.

'Where will the bee go' said Joe,
Back to heaven where little bugs go,
It's nice up there where the Earth is bare,
There's no one else around,
That's where the bee went when he hit the ground.

***Natalie Western (13)***
***Charlton School***

## CHRISTMAS TIME

It's Christmas time,
We all drink wine,
And sing merry songs.

When it's Christmas day,
We can't stay away,
From all the treats,
And delicious sweets.

I opened my eyes,
And in surprise,
There they were,
Like gold and myrrh.

Where do I start?
I said to my sister,
Under the tree,
But don't get a blister.

As I opened them,
One by one,
I think the best was from my mom.

I wish this day could always stay,
But tomorrow will be just another day.

***Laura Goode (12)***
***Charlton School***

## Me And My Sister

When I was born,
My sister was three,
I was crawling around,
On one knee.

My sister was six,
And I was three,
She never paid any
Attention to me.

We were in the garden,
Playing in the sand,
I fell over,
She wouldn't give me a hand.

My sister is fourteen
And I am twelve,
Nothing has changed
She is still the same.

***Claire Whitrick (12)***
***Charlton School***

## Family Poem

My folks are a bit batty.
My brother is daft.
My sister is mad,
but my mum and dad are really mad,
but me I am just the quiet one.

***Matthew Huda (11)***
***Charlton School***

## Hallowe'en

It's that time of year,
When ghosts appear,
The witches come out,
We scream and shout.

There are loads of black cats,
But they stink of rats,
Monsters creep around,
And slink along the ground.

We go trick or treating,
And witches go to meetings,
It is very, very scary,
And monsters are quite hairy.

But never mind, I'm not scared,
I'll go to sleep, I'm prepared.
Dracula flies in the night,
He bangs on the window and gives me a fright!

***Katie Leith (12)***
***Charlton School***

## Autumn Poems

Autumn is a peaceful season
with the wind blowing the leaves around.
All the brown conkers falling down on to the ground.
When you step on the leaves they make a crispy sound.
The wind blows swiftly while animals hide away.
The children shouting loudly as they pick
the conkers off the ground while they play.
As the heavy rain comes the children hide away.

***Danielle Rogers (12)***
***Charlton School***

## EDDIE

Hi, my name is Eddie,
When I was a baby,
My daddy changed my nappy,
I didn't like having my nappy changed,
It made me freak and run around,
Every time I ran,
He chased me with a nappy and Sudocrem too
Every time I did this,
He shouted at the top of his voice 'Nappy, nappy, nappy,'
At last he catches me,
To stick on my nappy,
First he takes off the old one (smelt a bit cheesy, phew!)
He sticks on the cream, which is as cold as ice,
Imagine an ice-cream going down your back,
Then he sticks on the new nappy,
It feels uncomfortable and weird too,
The only way to change the problem is to do another,
That's my story of nappy problems.

***Miriam Mhatab (12)***
***Charlton School***

## MORNING

The grandfather clock strikes seven in the morn,
my very day about to dawn.
My curtains are drawn and no longer hide,
the glories of morning emerging outside.

The glistening dew on the green, silken lawn,
the sullen sky, the clouds are torn.
Outside the workers head for their day's labour,
from the task, determined not to waver.

I move slowly downstairs to get set,
for the day ahead, not getting wet,
but in the classroom at my school,
the day new, the air cool.

The end of the day draws very near,
the weather comparatively now more clear,
bedtime comes, I shut my door,
and wait for morn to come once more.

***Steven Humbles (15)***
***Charlton School***

## My Best Friends

My best friends are great.
One of them is called Kate.
We play lots of games.
Another one's called James.
One's such a pain,
she's called Jane.
We all go to school
Jane falls off her stool.
She shouts out loud,
what a terrible sound.
We all go and play,
happily and gay,
what a lovely day.
Kate fell in some muck,
and became stuck,
she tried to get up,
but had no luck.

It's time to say goodbye,
I think I'm going to cry!

***Amanda Dovey (12)***
***Charlton School***

## WHY?

Why does the world tick by?
Why does time carry on?
Why do the seasons change?
Why do flowers blossom in spring?

Why do we hate things?
Why can't we love?
Why do we grumble?
Why not make the most of things?

Why does the sun shine?
Why do we need to know more about space?
Why can't it be left alone?
Why can't it be a mystery?

Why can't we remember dropping off to sleep?
Why do we dream?
Why do we have nightmares?
Why not think of better things?

Why do we eat and drink?
Why do we get hungry?
Why do people starve themselves?
Why do people get drunk, what makes them do it?

Why do people sit alone?
Why do people get picked on?
Why are people sad?
Why do we cry?

Who can answer all my questions?
Is it God, science or you and I?

***Fiona Carver (12)***
***Charlton School***

## THINGS I LIKE

T ennis, especially when I win
H ixxy, my dog
I ce-cream covered in chocolate sauce
N ot having any homework to do
G oing horse riding early on a sunny day
S wimming in the sea.

I cicles hanging from the roof.

L aughing with my friends
I ce cold drinks on a blistering hot day
K ite flying on an empty beach
E veryone of these things I like to do
with friends and family you can too.

***Anna Hubbleday (12)***
***Charlton School***

## DEVIL SHADOW

Shadow is a devil,
he's from another level.
Shadow's four years old,
a Hovawart I was told.
My dog's a trained sledge racer,
but he's more of a slow pacer.
Shadow's a naughty boy,
he chews up all his toys.
But whatever he does,
be it good or bad,
whatever he tries,
upon his treats, he relies.
He'll always be the cutest dog in the world!

***Victoria Clinton-Davies (11)***
***Charlton School***

## Animal Madness

My granny is a sweetie jar
she loves lots of chocolate.

My dog and cat drive us wild
and even I think it's wild.

My family came from Liverpool
now I've moved house
and people call us Scouse.

My house is wild, people blame me,
and me, I'm just the flea.

***Ben McLachlan (11)***
***Charlton School***

## My Sister Tara

My sister Tara
Ain't no joke
She'll even scare
A grown-up bloke!

Her wacky clothes style
She's a blister
Then again
Are you sure she's my sister?

When you want a job done
She'll always give it a miss
She's wild, wacky and stupid
But that's her ideal bliss!

***Ria Darricott (11)***
***Charlton School***

## NIGHT

Spreading and consuming life,
Closing on the unexpected,
Wrapping tightly around the insecure.

A thick, blue blanket keeping life safe.
A comfort to the strange.
A shadow to the creatures of the night.
A friend to the depressed.
A companion to the lonely.

Witchcraft happens at this time,
Rituals are performed under her protection.
All of this enters her conscious,
When stepping in her territory.

Pleasure can be dealt from her and received with gratitude,
Expectations can be taken and kept in solitude.

You can't touch her.
You can't sue her.
You can't injure her.

A lifelong sentence of ever rising,
A lifelong sentence of ever falling.
Forever persecuted,
Yet always remaining faithful.

***Felicity Jones (16)***
***Charlton School***

## THERE'S A MONSTER UNDER MY BED!

My sister says there's a monster under my bed,
With big green eyes and a great big head,
He comes out at night,
Because he hates the daylight,
When everyone's asleep and he's in the right mood,
He goes to our fridge to pinch some food,
My sister says he's really scary,
She says he's really big and hairy,
When I was in bed one cold night,
I had a really massive fright,
And from underneath my bed,
Popped this big and ugly head,
I looked at it and gave a scream,
The 'monster' had my tub of ice-cream!
My mum and dad came through my door,
And what a shocking sight they saw!
On the monster I noticed a blister,
That could only belong to my older sister!
Is that her who's played this trick?
I really feel like giving her a kick.

She had told a great big lie,
But what I want to know is why?

***Vicki Benting (12)***
***Charlton School***

## Redwall Abbey

Martin the Warrior
Bravest of the brave,
Bold and fearless
Never ever afraid.

He was the Warrior of Redwall,
His friends were all happy
Until the battle call
Reeeddddwwwalll!

They will fight for the Abbey
And the red stone wall.
Whatever size they come in,
Big, medium or small.

Good vs. evil
Heroes vs. the bad,
Martin the Warrior will fend all,
Even though he's not much past a lad.

After the heroes
Win the battle and the bloodshed no more,
The animals of Mossflower all cheer . . .
. . . Reeeddddwwwalll!

Now all that's left,
Of Martin the Warrior,
Is the spirits in our hearts,
And a tapestry upon the wall.

***Robert Schike (12)***
***Charlton School***

## When You Split One

You say black, I say white.
I'll pick a daisy, you'll pick a fight.

You are like the cold stark moon,
I am like the warm bright June.

I am love, you are hate.
You have little, I have great.

You stay home, I run free.
I am the gentle flower,
You are the stinging bee.

I say yes, you say no.
You wither, I grow.

You are the rain, I am the sun.
I smile sweetly,
Your tears run.

I am healed, you have pain.
You only lose, I only gain.

You say it's Sunday,
I say it's Monday.

I am the friend, you are the foe.
You are everywhere I go.

You are me, I am you,
Split one, you end with two.

***Kirsty Smith (14)***
***Charlton School***

## THE MATCH

It was our last chance
If we didn't win, we were going to sin
The score was nil, it was up to Bill
Then suddenly a roar, we just had to score.

They were winning
We were sinning
I had the ball, I passed it to Paul
He took it behind the goalie's box
And mud splatted his socks
Suddenly *goal* right from his soul.

It was one all, they had the ball
They had a go, but it was too low
I sighed, we tried
*Goal!* We won, we won.

***Hanna Kille (12)***
***Charlton School***

## THE CHEETAH!

It's the creature of beauty that can cause you such fear,
You tremble and sweat when a cheetah is near,
Swiftly the cheetah runs through the grass,
The grace of its body as it runs so fast,
The power of its movement as it pounces on its prey,
Down on the floor the victim will stay,
The sound of the prey's cries which make the herd flee,
The cheetah has its meal for all to see,
The cheetah will sleep, so quiet and serene,
Until it hunts again without being seen,
The cheetah so fearsome, so sly and so mean!

***Zoe Sadler (12)***
***Charlton School***

## My Auntie Sue!

My babysitter is very nice,
She brings us sweets, my favourite sugar mice,
Her back aches but she doesn't care,
She watches telly with us and brushes my hair.

My babysitter lets us stay up late,
She plays pirates with us, it's so great!
My little brother goes to bed at ten,
Then we go out partying, but come back again.

My babysitter goes really red,
When mum and dad come 'cos then I scoot off to bed,
I tell a fib or two,
About being minded by Auntie Sue!

***Julena Niehoegen (12)***
***Charlton School***

## Sweets

Sweets, sweets, lovely sweets
Minstrels, pastilles, they are treats.

Sweets, sweets, lovely sweets
Chicken, bacon, yuck! They are meats.

Sweets, sweets, lovely sweets
Fruit and veg I like the least.

Sweets, sweets, lovely sweets
I like biscuits, they are crunchy to eat.

But . . .

Sweets, sweets, lovely sweets
I like chocolate best as a treat.

***Laura Smith (12)***
***Charlton School***

## The Gloomy Mine

Walking miles through the abandoned streets
silent feelings travel up and down my spine
I feel the oozy air as I step into the mine
stepping into the deep, dark mine
I hear the gunpowder blow
in the distant chamber down below

I move silently
all I hear are the men's clogs slamming
the ground below me
All that goes through my mind is death
the darkness
as I leave my cart to carry some
more heavy black slate
I hear a bang, a scream then weeping cries

Abruptly I hear slamming boots again
feeling like I might be dead
Suddenly I hear a squeaky bell
we all walk half a league of hell

At last I am in the cage to freedom
with a sigh of relief
I look back to the gloomy entrance of the
dark, deep mine
head back home
then eat dry cake and go to bed
horrible images still in my head.

***Tahlia Lawson (11)***
***Charlton School***

## Roller-Coaster

*R*ound and round like the hands of a clock
*O*ver and under and twirling around
*L*onger and faster,
*L*onger and slower,
*E*very time getting higher and lower.
*R*ushing recklessly round the track.
*C*old, clean air blowing in my face.
*O*h no here we go,
*A*hhhhhhhhhh!
*S*creams of terror,
*T*otally frozen like a block of ice.
*E*ventually it ends.
*R*elaxing from the rowdy ride.

***Chris Stubbs (12)***
***Charlton School***

## My Family!

My brother is a pest
but sometimes he's the best!
My brother's name is Jack
he always gives me a whack!
My sister is a pain
when she sings she makes it rain!
My dad is such a laugh
he falls asleep in the bath!
My mum is such fun
she is such a good mum!
My family's such a whack
I would never give them the sack!

***Jillian Caton (11)***
***Charlton School***

## TIGER TIGER!

'Well here I am the tiger,
In the middle of the jungle no water,
No food, life couldn't be better!'

'I'm hunted most of the time,
and you know what,
I'm hunted just as I'm about to eat or kill food!
So they chase me in their snazzy new jeep,
Firing their rifles at me while I'm just running in bare feet!'

'When I finally lose them
I go for a spot of hunting myself,
Perhaps antelope, or a deer
and sometimes I get a really good meal from a warthog,
*Yummy!'*

'Eventually I take my kill back to the Mrs and kids,
Tear open the kill and feast
To our hearts' content.'

'After a hard day's work a tiger needs his beauty sleep
So I curl up and doze off.
At about sunrise I'm woken by a nudge
Dad, Dad I need the toilet.'

'And that's my life!'

***Justin Andree (11)***
***Charlton School***

## LITTLE V LARGE

I was deep in the jungle
scared out of my wits,
that I would fall
into cannibal pits.

I heard a rustle,
and looking around
there was a puma
patrolling the ground.

The puma seemed brave,
strong and slick,
along came a possum
and gave him a kick.

The puma screamed out,
and hid behind a tree.
The possum looked cheeky
and then off went he.

For several days
I hid in a tree,
afraid that the possum
might come and hit me.

***Michael Davies (12)***
***Charlton School***

## AUTUMN POEM

Leaves falling on the floor,
Leaves rustling in the trees,
Leaves silently flying in the sky,
Animals hibernating, dogs howling loudly,
People going for walks, seeing crispy leaves,
People wearing coats, gloves and thermals,
Conkers falling gracefully to the ground.

Trees howling softly,
Trees moving swiftly,
Nights going dark,
Days going cold,
Afternoons going drizzly and rainy.

***Stefanie Bott (12)***
***Charlton School***

## Where I Belong!

If I was to live in Jamaica,
I'd party all night and sleep lata,
But for me this is unknown,
I'd soon be left at home,
With a paper and jacket potata!

If I was to live in the US,
I'd be an actor and become famous,
But whilst acting in Hollywood,
I'd choke on some chud,
And suffer a cardiac arrest!

If I was to live in France,
I'd teach all the French to dance,
Whilst doing a beat,
I'd trip over my feet,
And in hospital look like a nance!

I'd rather live in the UK,
Than if I lived in the USA,
If I went to Italy,
They kick me to Sicily,
So I'll just stay at home OK!

***David Ross (12)***
***Charlton School***

## Sports

Netball is a game I dislike,
So instead I ride my bike.
Riding my bike can be fun,
But better still I love to run.
Running fast, running slow,
I think I might give tennis a go.
Tennis can be rather boring,
But in football you can do a lot more scoring.
Putting the ball in the back of the net,
It's not like canoeing, you get really wet.
Under the water it is really rocky,
So I think I'll go and play hockey.
But playing hockey was just like the rest,
Even though I had tried my best.
All of these I tried to do
I think I need to find something new.

***Sarah Collins (13)***
***Charlton School***

## Loneliness

Where are you tonight?
I wonder as I sit here in the light.
Will you ever come back to me?
I sit at home all alone, no one with me.
Do you ever think of me now?
If you do, I don't know how.
I miss your laugh
I miss your smile
But most of all
I miss you
Baby Niall.

***Lauren Austin (13)***
***Charlton School***

## AUTUMN

Golden leaves lie all around
damp and crushed upon the ground,
the trees are bare, naked now
hardly a leaf left on the bough.
The days grow short and the wind blows colder,
scarves round necks, draped on shoulder.
Fires are lit to bring some cheer,
Bonfire Night will soon be here.
Fireworks crackling, whizzing, booming
then before we know, it's Christmas looming.
Longing for a summer's day
wondering why it hides away.
Beneath the soil its buds lie sleeping
its beauty from our eyes it's keeping.
We know in triumph it will return one day
and chase the winter right away.
But for now the autumn reigns supreme
and summer is just a faraway dream.

***Rachael Beckett (12)***
***Charlton School***

## TIGER

It's true I'm fierce with stripes like fire,
And claws like razor sharp knives,
To end my prey's lives.
But there you go,
Cutting down my home,
And when it's gone where shall I roam?
So do me a favour and leave me alone,
So that I can hunt in my forest home.

***Rhys Rhobat-Baker (11)***
***Charlton School***

## AUTUMN

The conkers fall gently to the floor
and break the dark silence.
The shells crack on the solid floor.
The children collect them and take them to school,
while acting real cool.
The autumn breeze
makes children freeze,
they go inside and have some dinner
and get less thinner.
The leaves fall from the trees
and the fierce autumn breeze,
takes them through the air.
As fireworks boom
and Christmas looms
the people soon get excited.
They get loads of presents
and have a good time
even though the weather is not fine,
but soon the summer will be here
so have no fear.

***Kieron Hughes (12)***
***Charlton School***

## IN THE WOOD

Wasps buzzing all around,
Bugs crawling on the ground,
Birds singing, leaves dropping,
The sun is out the sun is shining.

The wind softly blows, the leaves
slowly moving.
Kids out having fun, running round
chasing butterflies.

The trees swaying to and fro
the man rows his boat row, row, row.

Squirrels running everywhere
dropping nuts on the floor
rustling through the long green trees.

***Ceri Machin (12)***
***Charlton School***

## AUTUMN

The wind was cold the ground was wet,
the autumn leaves hadn't fallen yet.
The conkers were hung high in the trees,
but were starting to fall off in the autumn breeze.
Frost-bitten toes and noses raw,
you could see that autumn was here once more.
The evening went the next day came
autumn was here for sure again.
Children playing in the leaves,
picking up conkers from the bottom of trees.
They crack open the shells,
the conkers shine like bells.
The children make holes and thread through string,
their faces full of excitement, what fun conker season brings.

Autumn is ending Christmas is near,
for sure autumn's gone for another year.
The evenings get colder the sky gets dark,
the autumn winds turn frozen and sharp.
Children stay in or else catch a cold,
winter is coming, and the joys that it holds.

***Sarah Duffett (12)***
***Charlton School***

## The Three Little Pigs

The three little pigs came out to play,
To have fun throughout the day.
The first little piggy built his house from sticks,
But then the wolf came out - up to his devilish tricks.
He huffed and he puffed and he blew the house down,
And sticks were scattered all around.
The second little piggy built his house of hay,
Then the wolf blew it away.
The third little piggy was rather bright,
So he built a brick house over night.
The wolf came out,
He acted very devout.
He tried to blow the house down in profanity,
And he eventually lost his sanity.
The wolf finally died,
And in joy, the piggies danced and thrived.

***Stuart Green (14)***
***Charlton School***

## Love Hurts

Love hurts,
But love hurts more when it hits you.
Boys are like rain, they come and go,
Like April showers and some are like snow.
God knows why he put them here,
Maybe he didn't, they just appeared,
But all I know
Is love hurts.

***Olivia Goode (11)***
***Charlton School***

# HONOURABLE MEN

Beneath the beautiful tranquil sky,
A thousand honourable men do lie,
The gentle hum of a solitary bee,
Flies through the ghastly stone white sea,
Only angels look upon this land,
Time washed them away like grains of sand,
Buried beneath foreign ground,
Where once they fought, now not a sound,
The tears shed could've drained the sea,
But now the only visitor is that solitary bee,
They fought and saw their friends fall dead,
Bullets and cannons flying overhead,
Now lying side by side,
The country wept, the country cried,
But nothing was gained,
Lives took in vain,
Corpses scattered all over the ground,
Some never even had their names found,
Now lush green grass grows overhead,
A pine wood box is their eternal bed,
So these honourable men have left our earth,
Gone before the day of our birth,
Yet the tide still comes in and out,
And dawn still has dusk, up and about,
Empty headstones without a name,
The field where they died will never be the same,
Gone to a better place, we pray,
They never lived long enough to see D Day,
These honourable men whom I so admire,
Now known unto God.

***Carys Jones (12)***
***Charlton School***

## AUTUMN POEM

Leaves falling on the ground,
different colours all around.
The wind howls and blows the leaves,
they swiftly float in the autumn breeze.
Kicking around the autumn leaves
rustling and crunching crisply.
Children play, laugh and shout,
messing with the leaves no doubt.
The wind is blowing through the trees,
that now hardly have any leaves.
We go inside where it's nice and warm,
we barge through the door in a big swarm.
Chips and beans on the table,
the baby's lying in the cradle.
We eat our tea then go to bed,
and then rest our sleepy heads.
In the morning we will get up and say
'It's just another autumn day.'

***Laura Perkins (12)***
***Charlton School***

## AUTUMN POEM

The autumn leaves blew off the trees,
they fell on the ground without sound,
then I saw a conker once more,
conker, conker come down,
autumn was definitely about.

I was walking and wandering about,
and something landed on my head with a clout
and rolled onto my snout,
it was a conker, a great big conker, without a doubt
that meant winter was about.

But we know that conkers would not be about
for long because winter was coming without a doubt.
We went inside where it was warm,
everywhere outside there were leaves floating about.

Women and children put on their wellies
and jump in the leaves with very big bellies,
run inside to clean their wellies,
autumn was definitely about.

***Oliver Allport (12)***
***Charlton School***

## THE BIRTH OF NATURE

Nature wanted to be born,
Nature wanted to grow,
It wanted to evolve.
It grew and grew,
Everything grew, sprouted and nature evolved.

Green was the shade.
Black was the darkness,
Colour sprouted and flowers shone,
Animals were born,
. . . and water came.

It twisted and turned and was clear,
It wanted a colour,
. . . but none was given to it.

So it stayed close to the ground in shame,
. . . and living things drank it.

Earth evolved, it arrived,
. . . it grew and made living things,
Its inhabitants.

***Kay Turner (13)***
***Charlton School***

## AUTUMN POEM

The leaves were rustling in the wind
There are green and brown and gold ones too.
People are dressing up in coats and gloves,
Men, women and children put on their winter clothes
And sweep up every leaf,
but over night they softly fall peacefully they land on the ground.
Hedgehog's tunnel into the leaves and then when they think it is time
they start to hibernate.
Conkers start to fall with a thud
Some kids have lost, some kids have won.
As children begin to sweep the leaves more begin to fall
As green leaves turn into golden leaves and crisp golden leaves turn
into dull brown leaves.
It looks like it is autumn not long till winter.

***Hannah Beeston (12)***
***Charlton School***

## CHOCOLATE

I love chocolate,
Chocolate chocolate,
It slides to your mouth
and down your throat,
Chocolate chocolate,
You cannot help getting some more,
Chocolate chocolate,
If I eat any more I will be as big as an elephant,
Chocolate chocolate,
I don't care,
    Chocolate
    Chocolate
    Is the best.

***Gemma Offland (11)***
***Charlton School***

## My Family Of Five

My family is five
we don't live in a dive.
We live in a home,
it's not shaped like a 'dome'.
My brother is nine
he's next in line.
I have one more
he is a little 'bore'.
My dad is a plumber,
I think he's a 'stunner'.
My mum does it all
she is so 'cool'.
My name is Rachelle
that says it 'all'.

***Rachelle North (11)***
***Charlton School***

## Dolphins

Dolphins are graceful, shiny and sleek,
Although they're not birds they all
have a beak.
They talk to each other through
oceans of blue,
With strange communications that
mean nothing to you,
They're kept in captivity why
I don't know,
I'd rather they lived in places
they know.

***Rebecca Horsewood (11)***
***Charlton School***

## AUTUMN POEM

Leaves all brown
They are going to die
When we play outside
We are saying bye bye.

Conkers come down
We pick them up
They bounce on our head
And then we shout 'Yup!'

Kids play out
And playing in the snow
Someone throw a snowball
And Percy shouts 'Oh no!'

Kids walking to school
Jack said 'What a drool.'
He bumps into a tree,
Hurts his knee,
And falls into a pile of leaves.

He plays around
With his conkers
Mom thinks
He's a load of bonkers.

***Ashley Rogers (12)***
***Charlton School***

## My Favourite Things

Snow on grass
Baubles made of glass.
My favourite player playing football,
Me and my friends having a ball.

I love the sound of cheering fans,
I am standing in a winter wonderland.
My favourite smell mince pies.
My favourite place the countryside.

The flavour of marzipan
My feet on wet sand.
My bed in the morning
The birds giving me a wake-up warning.

The smell and taste of candyfloss
and watching the Man U boss.
The smell of the sea
Boxing with Muhammad Ali.

Sitting next to a fire
listening to rustling water,
laughter, Christmas, chocolate and music.
I wish I could have all my favourite things at once.

***Sally Smith (12)***
***Charlton School***

## AUTUMN POEM

The brown leaves start to crisp
They drop to the ground and whip
The conkers fall down to the floor
I hear no shouts no screams no more

Children run around in the leaves
They look so happy and very pleased
The children's noses look so sour
I hear the noise of conkers falling to the floor

Children rush to the trees' ground
Little children go to the tree
But all of the conkers have been found
And all that's left are conker shells
And then we hear the 1 o'clock bells.

***David Biddulph (12)***
***Charlton School***

## STARS AND MOON

A dark night,
The stars are gleaming bright,
Small from the ground,
Not making a sound,
One whole moon,
It comes out far too soon,
A bright light,
Always in sight,
Surrounded by stars,
The moon follows all cars,
The morning has arrived,
The night has survived.

***Samantha Hand (11)***
***Charlton School***

## The Hunt

I'm running fast
The dogs are coming
I'll dive under a log
And they'll stop running

Oh no they've lit a fire
They're sending in a fox hound
I'd better find a way out
And hope that I get homeward bound

I can hear the protesters
Making the bugle sounds
But that's OK
Because they stop the fox hounds.

***Andrew Hayward (12)***
***Charlton School***

## Wind & Rain

W recks every house in sight,
I t gives you a nasty fright,
N oisy around my ears,
D estroys everything, everything is silent nothing left except a mess.

&

R ain can be rather rough,
A pril showers,
I nches when it pours,
N asty when it roars.

***Stacie Glover (12)***
***Charlton School***

## My Life As A Computer

My life as a computer
It's fun you see
People play on me
It doesn't matter to me.

They surf the net
They write to their friends
They play on me again and again
They draw pictures on me then
They go to tea and after that
They play on me.

After playing on me, they go outside
I feel alone, dark inside
And then two people come behind
It's Mom and Dad
Hip, hip, hooray, they're playing on me
Hooray hooray they surf the net all day.

My life as a computer was the best day
But we can play another day
But it's time to say goodbye
They turn me off
Oh no, oh no
bye.

***Richard Jackson (12)***
***Charlton School***

## VIOLENCE (LIFE)

People live, people die,
People get shot in the eye,
People shoot,
People cry,
People stab,
And people jab,
It all spells out the word 'life'.
'He got in the way of the gun,'
'He should be punished, it's not a game and
certainly isn't fun.'
You might die tomorrow, you might die today
So, what if people get shot.
Does it matter that Hitler was responsible for
killing five million?
Would it have mattered if it was five billion?
You see that the point I am trying to make,
Is the point about mankind's huge mistake,
We have evolved over millions of years,
Don't you think that we would be more
sophisticated after a few too many beers?
I'm not asking for people to be Gods
Just to act better than dogs.

***Andrew Holland (14)***
***Charlton School***

## THE OLD HOUSE

The old house stood still on the hill,
Groaning with the wind like an ancient old granny,
Ghosts wandering the halls, the dusty empty halls,
The windows smashed, like cups and saucers,
Scaffolding just standing there no one using it,
No one dared go near it for fear of the ghosts,
Abandoned, lonely on the hill,
No smile could the poor house smile,
The only visitors were rats and mice,
Stones being thrown at it every second of the day,
Scaring the poor house to death,
If the wind blew any harder it would fall,
Tiles falling off the roof making the poor house cry,
Cement falling and crumbling,
Birds making nests, blocking the gutter,
The house sighs on the hill,
It watches the cars zooming by,
And the birds in the sky,
How I wish that I could fly,
Fly away to somewhere where someone needs me,
The lonely old house cries on the hill.

***Jilly Sankey (11)***
***Charlton School***

## An Archer's Dream

The referee blows his whistle,
The competition's under way,
I'm feeling rather nervous,
Will I have success today?

The target stands before me,
Like a multicoloured wheel,
Nervous and excited,
That is how I feel.

I slowly pick my bow up,
From the firm solid ground,
And then before the target,
I take my stand.

I slowly raise my bow,
I draw back the string,
The arrow whizzes off it,
With a great loud ping.

It speeds towards the target,
Straight and bold,
My eyes light up with pleasure,
It's landed in the gold.

The competition's over,
The shooting's all being done,
I get a brilliant feeling,
When they tell me that I've won.

***James Beckett (12)***
***Charlton School***

## KIDS

Kids, kids, lots and lots of kids,
Riding on their bikes,
And pulling loads of skids,
Big kids, small kids,
Fat kids and tall kids,
Kids love crisps and chocolate bars too,
They also enjoy a visit to the zoo,
Wherever kids go they always have fun,
Kids can never walk, they always have to run,
They love to play on swings, in the park,
They annoy little dogs and make them bark,
Kids love to jump, and play and have fun,
And when it comes to night
They play 'knock a door run'.

***Scott Moffat (12)***
***Charlton School***

## ON TIME

School starts at quarter to nine,
Better run to be on time,
Can't be late on my first day,
I hope I don't lose my way.

Into the school I do rush,
It is just a big, mad, crush,
And up the stairs I do race,
Trying to miss Teacher's face.

Registration starts right now,
I've scraped in, I don't know how,
My name is just shouted out,
'Hooray, I'm on time,' I shout.

***Ruth Walmsley (12)***
***Charlton School***

## SPAIN

Spain is so beautiful in my eyes
Please let me go again.
I'll see the sparkling, blue sea and get
Buried in the soft sand.
Anger strikes me when my parents say
'No you can't go' but I understand when we
Have just been, so you have probably
Gathered I love *Spain.*
Now I really like to go to see the seagulls
Squawking, flapping and pinching food
from small children.
Every day I would sunbathe on the beach
Swimming is what I love to do in the
Perfect, deep, blue sea.
Animals, I love the animals such as the gulls
It is so perfect in *Spain,*
Now I know I want to go again.

***Amy Turner (11)***
***Charlton School***

## SCHOOL

Every day you go to school
Even though the teachers are cruel
The school dinners taste like gruel
And they make you stand outside to look a fool.
They make you play boring games like boules
And use you as a technology tool.
When you do a practical, Teacher says 'Don't sit on that stool!'
When hometimes comes, you ride away on a mule,
And when you get home, you play pool.

***Matthew Keeler (14)***
***Charlton School***

## DREAM

I wander through my dreary dream,
And think of what it could mean.

A crowd of people,
A busy town,
And in the middle is me.

What am I doing,
Am I thinking,
Am I lost,
It doesn't make sense to me.

A crowd of people,
A busy town,
And in the middle is me.

I look at all the people,
They will not relax,
Sit down for a chat,
It doesn't make sense to me.

A crowd of people,
A busy town,
And in the middle is me.

***Sarah Timms (12)***
***Charlton School***

## THE SHARK

See how he swims through the deep blue water,
Swimming beside his little proud daughter,
Searching for food in the dead of night,
Never has he lost a fight.

Gripping,
Biting,
Tearing,
Fighting,

See how he dives through the deep blue sea,
Looking out for a feast for tea,
Teeth as sharp as a butcher's knife,
Better watch out! He'll take your life.

Gripping,
Biting,
Tearing,
Fighting,

All the sea life without a notion,
He's searching for you in the deep dark ocean,
When he takes you down to the murky floor,
You can safely say you will be no more!

***Lindsay Harvey (12)***
***Charlton School***

## Summer Sea

At the sea the waves crash like cymbals
crashing together,
Bubbly blue sea,
As blue as the sky on the sunniest of days,
The sea sounds like a tiger roaring in a storm.
The sea goes calm,
Then with a huge roar it rushes against the rocks,
The water changes to beautiful shades of blue and green,
It crackles gently on the rocks.
Screaming, splashing everybody loves the sea,
When it returns to its normal position
the sand is flat,
Until that cruel person digs their footprint in,
The sea is powerful!

***Ruth Swift (11)***
***Charlton School***

## Wolf

The she wolf full of milk,
The cubs so full of play.
Their coat like shimmering silk,
She watches them all day.
She hunts to keep them strong,
They eat and grow so fast.
She corrects them when they're wrong,
But knows it will not last.
One day they'll go away,
Have a pack to lead alone.
So she'll smile and be happy one day,
When they have children of their own.

***Daniel McKiernon (12)***
***Charlton School***

## In a Girl's Head

In a girl's head there are . . .

Money trees and shopping sprees
Boys galore ice-creams more more
Everything goes with a flow.

In a girl's head there are . . .
Moonless moons and broken legs
Giant sunflowers and bigger pegs.

In a girl's head there are . . .
Lots of sun and late nights
Ace cars and flashing lights.

In a girl's head there are . . .
Screaming babies smashing plates
Ace clothes and cool mates.

All I know that in a girl's head
It's a big dream and I love it.

***Ruth Johnson (11)***
***Charlton School***

## FOREST FIRE

The immense heat,
And pounding of feet,
Fleeing from the fire,
Everything lost,
We've paid the cost,
Terror of the fire,
Fires burning,
Stomachs turning,
Corpses of the fire.

The humans caused it, burning the fields,
They didn't pause to think about others' needs,
Will they think of the consequences?
Guilt won't hold them in any fences.

They're not restrained by what they've done,
Will they ever stop?
Do they ever think of others,
Or does the world revolve around them?

Barren land of ashes, deathly land of corpses.

*Forest fire, death rate higher.*

***Anna Garvey (12)***
***Charlton School***

## A Life As A Flower

I'm a flower, straight and tall,
But some of us are very small.
My petals, big and colourful,
Which makes people bright and joyful.

My friends are flowers too,
Some red, some white, some blue,
I myself am purple,
And my petals go around an orange circle.

A yellow and black bumble bee,
Sometimes comes to visit me.
He takes my nectar and in return,
He gives me pollen which I yearn.

I was once a strapping seed,
But now I am a worthless weed.

***Cheryl Strang (13)***
***Charlton School***

## MY SECRET PLACE

I never assumed of such a beautiful place,
Which you wouldn't call petite
Because it has so much space.
Sun, sea and sand,
And lots of countryside land.
This place I can hardly describe,
Laughter, fun and having great fun
Even doctors can't prescribe.
Mountains, trees and rivers
A perfect paradise you never imagine to see,
For it's not for anyone but just for me.
As I lie looking at the moon's face,
It's not a dream this is true
For it's my secret place!

***Zabina Bibi (12)***
***Charlton School***

## THE LIONESS

Lurking in the shadows,
Hidden by the grass,
A lioness is stalking,
Around the misty marsh,
Her eyes sweep the water,
Like a fiery flame,
Any animal there
Will surely be her game.

***Laura Ockenden (11)***
***Community College***

## Riva's Walkies

It's 7 o'clock, who needs alarms?
My dog is all it takes,
To get me up each morning,
She barks till my head aches!

It's raining, get the wellies out,
Raincoat and her long lead.
Then it's to the brook we wander,
Our company's all we need!

Down the brook I throw her sticks,
We're always having fun.
She jumps in the water, I get soaked,
Then dry off in the sun!

***Adam Rose (12)***
***Idsall School***

## The Shoulder Bag

The bully is a shoulder bag
Slung nonchalantly off the shoulder of his gang.
The thoughts are stuffed inside him,
Until the clasp undoes itself.
The compartments are emptied like his brain,
My pride is zipped up and forgotten.
His hand is the leather strap
Whipping me until I am leather black and suede blue.
I am shut away to the world,
Until I can hold my pride once again . . .

***Penny Corp (12)***
***Marches School***

## His Face

Looking at his face,
I see a compound of emotions.
Deadpan. Hunted. Smug. Victorious.
This hard skull hides many secrets.
Maybe he should be stood up,
Applauded, given a well-done bouquet.
Maybe he should be locked in the cellar,
Given only air and water,
Left to his undying shame.

His once sharp eyes are half senseless,
One like a black bead,
The other, a half-wrapped moon.
His lips, two reddened bars
That tremble but never meet.
Mesmerised I watch him.
I want to ask him a world of questions,
But misfortune has taken his hearing.
I will never know his pain.

The only thing he can do is wish.
Wish that I would end his misery,
Wish that I could take his place, just for a moment.
Looking at his face,
I see a face no longer with a life on it.
I see a poor man's greystone grave
And a red flower every Armistice Day.

***Alice Stone (14)***
***Marches School***

## THE GRAVEYARD

They sit there standing in time
frozen souls locked in the ground
the cold plates of stone
inscribing the life
its soul below the dark crow of shadows
hunts its prey of light

people forgotten
people stand there
leaning in death the smell of fear
fills air of its evil intentions
spiders bugs crawlers
creeping through the long thin spiky grass
the dead flowers wither away
dying
withering

soon the cape of night does come and rest upon this world
and the crow of shadows comes to eat the dying daylight

the old church stands there falling away
the cold black stone in these walls
carries hope and life
and in the radiance of God and the fires of hell
do burn these wandering souls

death to life
life to death
the souls do wander this ground
mourning weeping crying
mournful to the life they had
and soon the lion of light does come
to bring them another day
in this old old graveyard.

***Kirk A Beard (14)***
***Marches School***

## THE BULLY IS A PENKNIFE

The bully is a penknife
cunning and cutting with the
spite of her blades that
stab me in my back.
With all of its gadget girls
all ganged together who
open my can of hurt
who cuts out my happiness
and she has the key to my weakness.
She twists out my hope
and serrates out all of my joy.
I am alone in my corner
she pulls me back out
and forces me into her
pocket of hate.
But my body is in pain,
and my guts being twisted with
the end of her tongue in
spite of me.
For some days I just wish
she could be put into the rain
to rust.

***Julie Gibson (12)***
***Marches School***

## THE CHIMNEY

The chimney stands unsteadily
as solemn as a battlefield
once the battle has been won or lost

A pile of scruffy bricks built up tall
greys, browns and oranges like rotten autumn leaves
shadowed by the oak tree of time

It has no use
like that dodgy Christmas sweater left lying around

If you get close you can almost taste
the rotting decades wasting away

There is a certain uncertainty about it
like an almost complete card castle
will it fall or won't it?

It leans just like the Tower of Pisa
but surrounded by empty cans and smashed bottles

It has the long shadow of a slow slithering slow worm
Creeping up the hill

The moss creeps up its side
like the smoke of a smouldering fire

It stands alone
a forgotten child

The chimney.

***Wayne Young (15)***
***Marches School***

## The Rosebush Of Pain

The bully is a rosebush,
With petals soft as silk,
The petals do deceive you,
Only blooming with his gang,
Which boosts his power to hurt.
But underneath the scented flower,
Lie the insulting thorns,
They hurt and prick my feelings,
My confidence has burst,
The sharp leaves pierce my skin.
His punches feel like nails,
Which sting me.
When it rains he grows,
My tears are the rain,
The seeds blow away and spread
More bullies. What a thought!

***Ben Sutcliffe (12)***
***Marches School***

## Dishing The Dirt

I'm Sue the sexy satellite, 'bit of a dish',
With my Gucci white coat.
I wear Chanel 4.
The Cable Guys try to flirt with me,
In a Jim Carey on.
I eat signal soufflés and frequency fries.
The gods from above try to stop me mixing with the wrong waves.
Carl Ton drops in sometimes.
But my gran, Ada doesn't like him.
So we are secret Friends.

***Jamie Horne (12)***
***Marches School***

## My Mate

My mate is a hero hammer
He's a football fanatic
He's a real cool reader.
As he dribbles down the road
The cars wipe their eyes in amazement.
He looks up to the sky
But will never get there.
He's so small
The smallest germs are giants to him.
He is a secret weatherman
Keeping cloudy secrets.
A twisting tornado
Won't open him up.
My mate is funny
His laugh carries on like
James Bond with the girls!

***Ben Hampson (13)***
***Marches School***

## Butter

I am the butter
And I fancy Marge
Even though she cheeses me off.
The cream has gone 'green' with envy
And the yoghurt has gone 'off' in a storm.
I'm usually the hardest in the fridge
But the microwave soon softens me up.
People call me a yellow bellied block-head
But I am Lord of the lard
The Monarch of Milk
The King of the cream.

***Oliver Dix (12)***
***Marches School***

## MIRACLE MIRROR

I am the miracle mirror
I hang about with the wall

I met this mirror image of me yesterday

I try to be sincere
but people seem to see straight through me

The picture frame across the room
thinks I'm two faced
but if I could swipe I'd give him a right shiner

I read the clock's times
though sometimes it really ticks me off

For meals I eat Perfecteo Polish
but always end up with dusty dessert

At night I snuggle up to the dark
it frames me with a twilight kiss.

***Daniel Ryng (12)***
***Marches School***

## The Tale Of A Wondrous Car Sprayer

I am a robot car sprayer.
I work all day in Frederick's Auto Cars
I am a spin doctor, patching up the scratches and filling the holes.
I pee on the cars as they go by.
I am now going out with a big hot air gun.
Her rays make me feel all warm.
She will be wearing Oil of Ulay or maybe it will be
Vaseline Intensive Care.
We will be munching on nutritious micro chips with a thick
spreading of olive oil on top.
At work the conveyor belt's stories are often very moving.
And the electrode welder really melts my heart.
The glass panes in the window often try to lie but they are seen
straight through.
The jack is trying to lift a van on the FORD (Fraud of Omega
Reorganised Distribution)
But we all say that machine labour will win in Accelerates court.

***Tom Elmitt (12)***
***Marches School***

## EMOTIONS

I sing of death, mouth-drying mustard
Burns my throat, as the organ plays
The slow march
Blood-freezing icicles prick my hand
The throttling smell of musty books,
Tortured faces stare through agonised eyes
Into my own.

I sing of hate, the musket fires,
My eyes sting as I choke upon
The petrol fumes released
By a punching fist,
A dagger gleams before
Lashing at my throat.

I sing of hope, a comforting embrace,
Birds sing sweetly in the tree-boughs,
A gently sucked boiled sweet
Envelopes my tongue,
A shaft of light pierces the
Looming clouds,
Freshly-baked bread is broken
And my nose alerts to it.

***Siôn Stedman (14)***
***Marches School***

## My Mate

My mate is a swimming maiden,
She'd love to swim the sea.
My mate is head over heels in love with Boyzone,
She'd eat them up for tea.
My mate is really pretty,
The shops just whistle at her.
My mate is a secret magnet,
As once you've told her a secret they're hard to pull away.
My mate is like a piece of rope,
She bends backwards and forwards.
I'm glad I've got a friend like Sarah,
'Cos, I'd be lost without her otherwise.

***Samantha Mirczuk (13)***
***Marches School***

## Tutankhamun's Death Mask

Staring, glaring,
Gaping, gawping,
His eyes stare into space,
He might wonder which king took his place,
He's sad, distressed and even bored.
He thinks about the snake who slithered
and the eagle who soared.
His head dress gives him an exotic look,
His nose is slender and diminutive,
His beard is wonderful and so straight.
It's disappointing that his life was took.

***Samuel Spencer (11)***
***Market Drayton Junior School***

## I Want To Be A Cat

I want to be a cat,
And stay at home all day,
And talk to other cats,
In a catty sort of way.

I want to be a cat,
And run around the place,
With paws, claws and a tail,
And whiskers on my face.

I want to be a cat,
Life would be so easy,
Play in the garden,
With the air cool and breezy.

I want to be a cat,
With long glossy fur,
I'd be the centre of attention,
With my comforting purr.

I want to be a cat,
With a life filled with fun,
Mouse chasing and leaf catching,
With lots of space to run and run and run!

I want to be a cat,
With no worries to be met,
With exception of
The white-coated *vet!*

***Jenny Collyer (13)***
***The Corbet School***

## Bud-Like

Bud-like, sprouting,
Growing, shouting,
Colours, beginnings,
Spring and new life.
Opening,
Flourishing,
Faded, older,
The peak, the climax,
Summer and life.
Losing, falling,
Shrinking, dull,
Rustic, endings,
Autumn and closing.
Ending, dying,
Frozen, still,
Cold, termination,
Winter and death.

***Laura Errington (13)***
***The Corbet School***

## No Punctuation Or Grammar

a poem with no punctuation or grammar is like a
fishing rod with no line
like a sweet with no sugar
like a work of art with no paint
likereadingasentencewithnospaces
its hard to catch a fish with no line
and its hard to visualise a work of art with no paint
and itshardtoreadthissentencewithnospaces
and its hard to read this poem with no punctuation or grammar

***Georgie Doyle (14)***
***The Corbet School***

## Dishes

Having to wash the dishes 'does me head in!'
'Have those dishes been washed yet?' your mother would shout
up the stairs
'No, I'll do them in a minute!' is a popular answer.
But what you'd really like to say is,
'Why don't you do them yourself,
You make the mess by cooking the tea,
You never do them, but always complain that they're never done!'
But, oh no,
You can't speak to the boss like that,
That will never do!
You have to do everything your mother says!

But the worse thing is washing dishes,
It gets your hands all wrinkly,
Your nails go soft,
And trying to scrub the grease off the baking tray from
yesterday's supper,
It takes ages to get it clean!

Having to wash the dishes 'does me head in!'
From this day forward I'm never going to wash a single dish
ever again!
'Have those dishes been washed yet?'
'No, I'll do them in a minute!'

***Jenny Owen (13)***
***The Corbet School***

## The Death Of A Forest!

Where has all the rain gone?
Where are all the trees?
The forest lies quiet,
Where once fell leaves.

Where once was colour,
And sunshine and light,
All is in darkness,
Both day and night.

No sound to be heard,
The silence is daunting,
No animal cries,
Add to its haunting.

Where has the rain gone?
Where are all the trees?
The forest has died,
Killed by human greed.

***Gemma Dean (13)***
***The Corbet School***

## Moonshine

Silver shimmers on the rippling pond,
His fluorescent trails touching the highest treetops,
He causes silhouettes on the vast grey ground,
His dominance threatened by impending dawn.

***Vicky Cooke (13)***
***The Corbet School***

## AUTUMN

Autumn days, long and weary,
Sparkling dew, icy cold.
Leaves shimmering in the sun's rays,
Reflecting gold in the morning sun.

Crunch crunch on the ground,
Cats and dogs scamper around.
Glittering cobwebs show the path,
Spiders spin around their home.

The sun goes down slowly,
The air turns damp and cold.
A mist comes down across the field,
Animals shiver and scurry home.

The moon and stars appear,
Covering the world in light.
Jack Frost returns and claps his hands,
Nothing escapes his touch.

At last it's done,
He stifles a yawn.
Silence stretches until it's dawn,
All that's left is a frosty world.

***Jenny Wilson (13)***
***The Corbet School***

## FEAR

Once upon a quiet time,
A vision came to me
Half asleep, I was that night,
So difficult to see,
Across the room
And through the night.

I pulled the covers to my face
And covered up my head.
This spirit - very much alive
Moved towards my bed.
So silently it crept about
Getting closer and closer, without a doubt.
Fearful then, I cried out,
Suffocated by its power
What lasted a minute, seemed an hour.

***Alex Gregory (14)***
***The Corbet School***

## What Is Life?

What is life?
Friends, family, hate and love.
The almighty power that lives above.
To eat, to breathe, to move, to grow.
Thinking, which direction my life will go.
Do we have a purpose on this Earth?
To take our time here for all it's worth.
Or is our purpose just to die?
As we wait we watch the years drift by.
Maybe we're here for only one thing,
For true love to make our hearts sing.
To seek and find what will make you happy.
A partner, a job or changing a nappy.
Is life all about family and friends?
They help you through life's long bends.
They keep you safe, they keep you well
Or though sometimes life might seem hell.
Think to yourself when you're in strife,
Everyone's going through this thing called *life*.

***Clare Whitelegg (14)***
***The Corbet School***

## RAINBOW

Have you seen a rainbow bending in the sky.
It is red and yellow, pink and blue
Do you ever wonder why?
It starts on the ground and goes up in the air
And it finishes almost anywhere.
You often see them after a shower
They are always gone within the hour.
Where do they go to? No one seems to know
Do they go down to the river where the waters flow?
Do they hide in the clouds until the rain comes down?
Do they lay still in a field, wearing a frown?
Where do you go rainbow with your colours so bright?
The one thing that I do know is
That you are a wonderful sight.

***Jayne Lucas (13)***
***The Corbet School***

## THE TIGER

The tiger spots its prey like a hawk
Homing in on a mouse,
Crawls through the grass
Not blinking in case the antelope sprints,
It shoots at bullet speed,
Four on one,
Grabs the neck and tears the veins
Stops the blood pumping to the brain,
All four tigers after the mass kill
Will snarl in pride and rip
Limb from limb
But people say it's cruel to shoot
A tiger and sell its skin.

***Ben Niddrie-Davies (13)***
***The Corbet School***

## My World

A place of beauty and peace,
Not of ugliness and war.
A place for fun at least,
Not where life's a bore.
A place where there is only good,
Not where people commit evil.
A place where we can keep our forests and woods,
Not where we have to wake up to the stench of diesel.
A place where we can visit the unknowns of Mars,
Not the well-known cities like Kent.
A place where all the bad is behind bars,
Not where they can hurt the innocent.
A place where there is kindness,
Not where there is cruelty.
A place where there is togetherness,
Not where there is solitary.
A place where there is hope,
Not where there is doubt.
A place where we can cope,
Isn't that what it's all about?
A place where each child has a home,
Not where they live on the streets.
A place where each garden has a gnome,
Not where pollution reeks.
A place where each person has an education,
Not where they have no future.
A place where everyone has medication,
Not where they can be eaten alive by some bacterial creature.
A place like this would make my dreams come true,
And maybe yours too!

***Lindsay Andrew (14)***
***The Corbet School***

## ONE MAN

The flying grey of steeplechasing.
Tall, elegant as he flew past,
Light, and fluent in his strides,
Long intelligent ears flick back and forth.

Two miles was his best trip.
The Queen Mother Champion Chase,
The grey had a spring in his step,
He strode on casting a shadow on the rest.

Aintree racecourse, was his last race
By the ninth fence the flying grey
Laid down in the gloom
His large, sharp eyes closed for ever.

It rained that day and the next.
His memory still goes on.
This day and the next and forever
He brought sunlight to many people's racing.

***Naomi Offen (14)***
***The Corbet School***

## POLLUTION

'Without me nothing would live,
For I am the most valuable thing to life.
People wouldn't survive, trees would die,
Look after you, others and I.'
The Earth says.

'The pollution you present to me is phenomenal,
Nitrogen, carbon and sulphur gases,
All lead to my slow devouring death,
Help make me a better place to live on.'
The Earth says.

'All the gases you release up into me,
Kill my protection layer for you.
You kill me I kill you back, simple,
Let's co-operate and heal my broken skin.'
The Earth just managed to say.

'This is my world as well as yours,
Power plants help you but destroy me.
I provide you with all the correct ingredients,
And you turn them sour.'
The Earth had tried to say.

***Paul Lewis (14)***
***The Corbet School***

## THE CAT

The cat was fat
The cat was black
The cat was full of cold
It snuffled in from the night
Looking sad but bold

The cat was sick
The cat was ill
It didn't look too good
But friendly vet came along
Who made things look much better

The cat was fat
The cat was black
The cat was ill once more
Mum called the vet
Who said
Harry is Harriet.

***Shonagh Broad (14)***
***The Corbet School***

## The Rally

The cars arrive hoping to win.
Some of the cars will end up in a bin.
Some will start some will finish,
Some will fade and just diminish.

All the cars rev at the start
then the flag goes down and all part.
They all leave in single file
One hits a fence the other a stile.

The cars bound up and down
The drivers cheer and half the town.
The rally sprint starts, who is the best?
The Escort Cosworth just waits for the rest.

The race goes on day and night.
Each competitor prepares for a fight.
The night stage finishes in poor light,
The drivers tried with all their might.

The Cosworth won with flying colours,
The nearest one was Joseph Mullers.
One of the hazards was a ramp,
This fooled one driver who landed in a nudist camp.

***Matthew Holland (14)***
***The Corbet School***

## Top Of The World . . . ?

Going out this Friday
Gonna have a laugh
Two quid I'm gonna pay
Get some Guinness draught.

My life is on top
Watching days go by
Stressing 'cos my dad's a cop
Getting arrested, just tell a lie.

In the prime of my youth
Need some discreet bit of culture
Wanna be Australian, ah, strewth
Or could pick bones like a vulture.

Listen to some music, hard beat
Pay no attention in school
Gotta pick myself off my feet
Was sick last night, alcohol, what a fool.

Try to persuade it's a good time
But I know it's not going to plan
Try to think it's all going, well fine
Let me go back to when I began.

Need some help, I'm going down
No therapy, or physio can help
The waves of normality, choke till I drown
Can be beat till I scream and help.

***Mike Feast (14)***
***The Corbet School***

## AUTUMN DAYS AND NIGHTS

In the swirling east wind breeze,
All the leaves fall off the trees,
Yellow, red and sometimes brown,
These are all the colours left upon the ground.

While you're in the frost,
And the sun is lost,
Jack Frost comes out of sleep,
And out he goes to creep.

When the nights close in,
The hedgehogs live in the bin,
While the days draw shorter,
And the nights grow longer.

Birds fly to hotter lands,
Squirrels search for nuts upon the ground,
While spooks and ghosts
Scare the most,

Fruits and crops are gathered in,
Ready for the new year to begin,
Seeds of food have been sown,
Ready for the year unknown.

***Rebecca Evans (14)***
***The Corbet School***

## CONTACTING!

Your sharp eyes meet mine
our heart's acting like magnets.
The uncontrollable force pulls us together
the chemistry is working.
Everything is blurred - except you.
Your sweet smile warms me up
just as a glowing fire does,
releasing out words of heat and flames.
Your kindness reaches out towards me
gently touching my breathing heart.
My feelings which I want to express
dance around in my head.
My emotions run away to my mouth
the words of my heart pour out to you.
My emotions and feelings scatter and spray
over your mind and body.
Our souls hold each other tightly
feeling our warm breath
trickle over our cool bodies.
Happiness takes itself behind us
tenderly moving us closer.
Feeling the emotions sweep over
and the body heat.
Heart's pounding but nothing can
come in between us now.
Nothing can hurt us. . .
So glad our souls have reacted
and now it's love - as we've connected.

***Anna Rogers (14)***
***The Corbet School***

## A Windy Day

*The wind blew hard*
hurrying and scurrying down the winding lane.
Swirling and whirling leaves of all different colours.
Gold, red, bronze and orange
twisting and twirling on an endless journey.

*The wind blew hard*
huffing and puffing like a fierce steam engine.
Drifting and turning in all directions
racing as fast as they could
round and up and down like a carousel.

*The wind blew hard*
trees bending and straining, fighting the monster.
Branches tearing and screaming
in an endless dance.
Waiting for the next gust.

*The wind dies down*
leaves settle, exhausted from the battle.
Trees standing motionless resting
everything is suddenly still . . .
*Silence!*

***Andy Smith (14)***
***The Corbet School***

## A Poem About Nothing . . .

It was dark
there was not a sound.
It was full of air
there was a slight breeze.

Not a person
not an animal.
There was nothing
you could hear a penny drop.

No pollution
no air, no gases.
Just open space,
could be just about anywhere.

No moon or stars
no sun, not cold, not bold.
No cars, no planes,
no earth, no heaven.

Just nothing, nothing to be seen.
No birds in the sky.
No fish in the sea.
No sky . . . no sea.

*Nothing!*

***Stuart Price (13)***
***The Corbet School***

## TWO SHATTERED LIVES . . .

I want to break this . . .
Escape this, and twist this.
It's not that flexible -
it would shatter and fall.
This pathetic one
we watch and laugh and I
I know who you are . . . I have seen
in the mirror and through the storm.
You want to play, well here's your chance.
The smile is crude and patronising.
The lust is cool and tempting
the breath makes me wanna
scream but now reply, they know your
soul is tormenting and still.
Hold on to the walls, they could be breaching.
Is it fear while they're laughing.
Do they know - you know?
They know I'm cracking in my cyber world
the metal influence.
In the wind I hear
ribbons of colour invade in here.
Throw me the rope I am lost at sea
me - in the ocean
feel the plundering waves,
catch it sideways
glancing.

I can feel the pain, all alone, I can't see the light.
Love is the bitter sweet delight.
Can't grow up! Never be tamed!
Don't want to shine, no smell of fame.
I just want to break the glass that holds me
letting me survey . . .
but not allowing any physical connection.
Watch me . . . last resort is to pray!

***Freya Henderson (14)***
***The Corbet School***

## Our Saviour Day

The sun setting in the west,
Falling down like a treasure chest,
A collapsing goldmine in the sky
Sizzling silently as it takes its last breath.

Light falling overhead,
Like a shadow of the dead,
Darkness prevails demons of the night,
Fighting the break of dawn to save tonight.

A little glimmer in the sky,
A ray of light to break the demons of the night
A break of night to bring through day,
And send the evil demons away.

***Owain Willcock (14)***
***The Corbet School***

## POEMS!

Poems are easy, poems are hard
some are good, some are bad.
The hardest part when writing a poem
is what to write about!

What about this and what about that?
Don't put that, you'll sound like a prat!
Make it funny, me yeah right!
Oh Lord - what to write!

I need some good inspiration,
problem is writer's constipation.
Write about something small or something tall
how about nothing at all!

Something about a mystic creature?
Or something bad about your teacher.
Better not cause some tension
probably put ya in bloomin' detention!

Copy one out of a book,
there's no harm in having a look.
Knowing my luck
it'll be the teacher's favourite one.

How come some people find them easy,
mine always turn out so bloomin' cheesy.
I've never been good at poems
and I suppose I never will.

Starting - it goes pretty well
after that it's like bloomin' hell.
What to put at the end
this is making me go round the bend!

***Mark Davies (13)***
***The Corbet School***

## The Death Of A Tree

I am a bird, I fly around.
Making a sweet chirping sound.
I live in a nest, in a tree
I do not like what I see.
I see the death of a tree.
It's horrible, it's sad to see.
The chain saws make an awful sound,
the noise echoes throughout the ground.
The tree is taken, taken away
on this very tragic day.
Its siblings surround it one by one,
then suddenly the tree is gone.
My habitat destroyed, no place to go,
for I am only a young sparrow.

I am a lumberjack, I cut down trees
with the greatest of ease.
Thousands of trees a day
it gives me my pay.
Listen the tree stood alone for many years,
and though it's now gone don't shed your tears.
It's had a life much longer than man,
and has seen much more than most people can.
Even though it's dead and gone,
the wood from trees lives on and on.
It might be used to make a door,
some furniture, or even a floor.
Burning wood helps to ward off chill.
So that felled wood has a usefulness still.

***Alison Wright (13)***
***The Corbet School***

## THE SPELL

Gather here us witches three,
all around the oak tree.
Visiting here from the depths of hell
here we come to cast this spell.

Scream, shriek, screech, cackle,
all the children we do tackle.
Fast asleep in their beds this night
on them we pounce to give them a fright!

To cast this spell all we need,
is to pull up some plants and make things bleed.
And we have the intelligence,
to put in our cauldron these ingredients.

Saliva of a cat
Mucus of a bat.
Vocal chords of a dog
And warts of a frog.

Eyes of a lizard
Beard of a wizard
Vomit of a gnat
And entrails of a rat.

Venom of a cobra snake
to make your bones shiver and shake.
A pint of blood from a newborn child
and a large poisoned mushroom
that grows in the wild.

Finally to complete this curse
us three harridans do converse.
The charm is strong and the moon is high
by Friday morning . . . each child will die!

***Steph Thompson (14)***
***The Corbet School***

## Fred

My hamster is called Fred
he eats like he's never been fed.
Drinks, eats and goes to sleep
until at night when out he creeps.

Squeaking round the wheel goes
sniffing for treats with his brown and white nose.
Running up and down his cage
I jump out of bed in a rage.

'Shut up! Shut up!' I will say
Some of us have school the next day.
A couple of seconds with no noise
then out he comes with his toys.

My hamster is fluffy and sweet
but when he's hungry he'll have anything to eat.
He's bitten most of my friends
but that's nothing a plaster can't mend.

He runs around in his ball
bumping into everything including the walls.
The ball has split and he's running around in the house.
He stops and greets a friendly mouse.

***Becky Morris (14)***
***The Corbet School***

## Twins

Here's a baby, here's another
A sister and her infant brother.
But which is which - it's hard to tell
but I think Mother should know them very well!

***Varinder Singh Jagpal (11)***
***The Orleton Park School***

## When I Grow Old

When I grow old my hair will go grey.
When I grow old I will have false teeth.
When I grow old my skin will go wrinkly.
When I grow old I will moan.
When I grow old my memory will go.
When I grow old I will lose my sense of style.
When I grow old I will have to wear slippers.
When I grow old I will have to wear a plastic rain hat.
When I grow old I will have to look for all the bargains.
When I grow old I will have a trolley on wheels.
But worst of all . . . I will still be getting older!

*No one wants to get old.*

***Rowann Bowcutt (11)***
***The Orleton Park School***

## Autumn

Wind blows violently
Crisp, crunchy leaves underfoot.
The cold months begin.
Harvest Festivals arrive.
Let's collect the leaves . . .

Darkness comes early.
The wind rustles though the trees.
Ground has a new carpet . . .

***Claire Smart (11)***
***The Orleton Park School***

## WHEN I GROW OLD!

When I grow old in years to come
I'll think back about all I've done.
From a young man growing up
my life an overflowing cup.

Full of ambitions, promises and dreams.
Life in me just bursting at the seams.
Outside I look like an old me
but that is just what you see.

Inside I'll still feel a young boy,
wanting to play with the latest toy.
I don't want to sit in slippers and sleep
I want to be out and about on my feet.

Why does everyone think I can't hear.
No one says 'Come on mate, fancy a beer!'
I'm not dead yet, I don't think
so how about taking me for a drink?

I'm not ready for bowls or bingo
flat caps, a pipe and all that stupid lingo.
Of two fat ladies, and legs eleven
key to the door and that lucky seven!

So I might be old and wrinkled and bent,
but I'm not ready to be heaven send.
Every day should be lived as if the last
and not spent looking into the past . . .

***David Anderson (11)***
***The Orleton Park School***

## Just As I Get Older

Just as I get older losing my hair
riding round town in a wheel chair.
With a patchwork quilt across my lap
occasionally taking a quick little nap.

With a flowery frock
and a wrinkled stocking.
Sitting at home knitting a sock
comfy in a chair that's made to rock.

With flowers on the walls
and a rug on the floor.
I can hear a neighbour call
It might be Mrs Gillimore
from number ninety four!

***Melissa Davies (11)***
***The Orleton Park School***

## When I Grow Old!

When I grow old I'll have grey hair
I'll wear pink, fluffy slippers.
I will stop and chat to other people
My feet would ache but I'll still walk.

When I grow old I'll have grandchildren
I would have to waste money on chocolate.
I'll have to say how cute they are,
But really they are ugly!

***Stacey McAdam (11)***
***The Orleton Park School***

## When People Grow Old . . .

When people grow old they get very cold.
They should wrap up warm
Just like a new born.
Their hair grows white
Just over night.
*Oh! What a shame*
*No one to blame.*
It's all the worry
Always in a hurry.
They need to sit still
And make a will.
*Oh! What a shame*
*No one to blame.*
So very kind
But nearly blind.
Keep taking the pill
When they get ill.
*Oh! What a shame*
*No one to blame . . .*

***Phillip Walters (11)***
***The Orleton Park School***

## Autumn

Wind is whirling round
Leaves spinning, swirling past
*All different colours . . .*

***Rachel Price (11)***
***The Orleton Park School***

## When I Grow Old . . .

When I grow old I'll have to push tartan
shopping trolleys round the town.

When I grow old I'll have to wear cardigans
and fluffy slippers that cost one pound.

When I grow old I'll have to tell stories.

I'll have to say to children 'Haven't you grown!'
and give them sweets like people do.

Knit all day long . . .

Once we've grown old we'll stop
in streets and chat to strangers.

When I grow old wrinkles
will take over my face.

When you grow old you remember your childhood
like catching snowflakes on your tongue.

Now you're getting older . . . you begin not to care!

***Sarah Lewis (12)***
***The Orleton Park School***

## Bats!

Hamster like body
Moves swiftly through the night sky.
Sycamore seed ears.
A nocturnal animal
Flying through the sky at night
*The soft silky bat!*

***Gemma Anslow (11)***
***The Orleton Park School***

## When People Grow Old

When people grow old they start pulling shopping carts
down the rough roads.
They rock away on their old rocking chairs,
Listening to the news or reading the newspaper.

They shout people's heads off
if you don't let them have peace.

They also have walking sticks curved from the top
to keep the neighbours' pets away and leave them in peace.
If they ever come near they use them as a bat
they whack them hard and slow
and flying they go - without any bruises.
In their bed safe and sound.

*So this should be a warning to you all!*

***Anesa Matlub (11)***
***The Orleton Park School***

## When I Grow Old

When I grow old
I won't have to pay for a haircut
because I'll have no hair to cut!
I'll have little kids call me Grandad!
I'll drive to town in my electric wheelchair.
I'll buy anti-wrinkle cream.
Pop into Kwik-Save and then drive home.
To be greeted by cries of grandad, grandad!
*It's good to be old . . .*

***Jonathan Owen (11)***
***The Orleton Park School***

## When I Grow Old I'll . . .

When I grow old I'll . . .
Push around a trolley
and ride in a wheelchair.

I'll be covered with wrinkles
and carry a tartan bag.

*Why do I have to grow old?*

When you're old you want to be young
When you're young you want to be old.

*Why do I have to grow old?*

***Zahra Hussain (11)***
***The Orleton Park School***

## When People Grow Old They . . .

When people grow old they wear out of date slippers.
Pull tartan patterned shopping trolleys around.
They natter and chatter for hours on end
And on Sundays they go to bingo.

Wrinkles, dimples and grey fading hair.
Hair dye, anti-wrinkle cream and soothing candles
All part of a fabulous make-over!

They adore children and spoil them rotten
Memories and photos of a lifetime . . .

***Lauren Davies (11)***
***The Orleton Park School***

## LEAVES HAIKU

Leaves blowing from trees.
Dark nights are finally here
Howling wind . . . I fear!

***Michael Simcock (11)***
***The Orleton Park School***

## HAIKU

Leaves will fall swiftly
Making a golden blanket
Autumn days are here . . .

***Stephanie Turner (11)***
***The Orleton Park School***

## HAIKU

Leaves all golden crisp
Whistling wind blows swirling leaves
Fresh leaves hit the ground . . .

***Ian Dawes (11)***
***The Orleton Park School***

## AUTUMN HAIKU

Beautiful leaves sway
Blowing from the bright blue sky
Hitting land like bombs.

***Simon Oldcorn (11)***
***The Orleton Park School***

## WHEN I GROW OLD I'LL . . .

When I grow old I'll
pull round a trolley.
The wrinkles will run down my arms.

My hair will go grey
and fall out in clumps.
And my body will shrink
and fold and I'll creak.

My legs will go scaly
and rough.
My arms will go bony
and tough.
And my nose will go lumpy
and my ears all bumpy.
Oh! Why do I have to grow old?

Why do I have to grow old?
To face all the grey hairs and wrinkles.
And the creaking
And cracking of bones.
Oh! Why do I have to grow old?

On the outside
I'm old and wrinkly.
But on the inside I'm really quite young.
My bones may creak and crack
And false teeth
that clatter and chatter
*So what does age really matter!*

***Heather Stirling (11)***
***The Orleton Park School***

## When I Grow Old . . .

I'll be old and grey
I'll take my trolley out for the day.
I'll natter and chatter to old friends nearby
I'll do what I want - before I die.
I'll be blind and wrinkly before I know it.
I'll listen to my grandchildren read about a poet.
Then I'll remember the olden days
And think to myself . . .
*Oh! How I wish I was young again!*

***Rhiannon Worrall (11)***
***The Orleton Park School***

## When I Grow Old . . .

When I grow old I'll be bold
When I grow old I won't be told
When I grow old I'll be cold
When I grow old I'll hold gold.

***Gurjit Bdesha (11)***
***The Orleton Park School***

## Haiku

Golden crispy leaves
Drifting slowly from above
Drifting slowly down . . .

***Beckie L Morrey (11)***
***The Orleton Park School***

## When I Grow Old . . .

When I grow old I will hopefully just look old
And still be young inside.
So instead of playing bingo and golf
I will play football, rugby and other exciting sports.

You won't find me with an old tartan trolley
But a sports car full of expensive goods.
In my car you won't find suits and posh shoes
but sports clothes and trainers.

Unlike other old people wearing spectacles and false teeth.
I will wear designer shades and my own strong teeth.

If my grandchildren need baby-sitting
I will take them for the time of their lives.
To theme parks and cinemas galore.

But just to keep the old tradition going
I will still buy boring scarves and socks
For Christmas and birthdays.

*Just so I can have a laugh . . . !*

***Simon Del-Manso (12)***
***The Orleton Park School***

## When I Grow Older . . .

When I grow older I'll grow grey hair
When I grow older I'll be nicknamed *the old chap!*
When I grow older I'll wear a flat cap
When I grow older I'll wear tatty clothes
When I grow older I'll be young at heart
When I grow older I'll hopefully be as fit as a fiddle . . . !

***Neil Prescott (11)***
***The Orleton Park School***

## Boys!

Boys are pains
They drive me insane.
I may as well talk to the wall.
They shout and scream
And always daydream.
I don't see the point at all.
They try to be funny -
And if they've got money . . .
They think that they're on top of the world.
They never shut up
They just like to make a fuss.
And if they *are* quiet - it's because they're eating!

Boys are all the same -
They are complete pains.
That's the only thing they are any good at being!

***Emma Silcock (11)***
***The Wakeman School***

## Boys!

Boys - they think they're so hard
But they're just a big lump of lard.
Some think they're great
But they just end up in a state.
But most teachers end up with the bait
And boys are not my best mates . . .

***Jennifer Spray (11)***
***The Wakeman School***

## HERE WE GO . . .

Everywhere you go they're there.
Making snide comments about your figure or your hair.
Shouting or fighting around each corner you go.
*Then you think to yourself . . . here we go!*

There are a sensitive few who really do care.
But that species are generally rare.
The mention of *love and relationships* - oh no!
*Then you think to yourself . . . here we go!*

My advice is to give 'em a scare
Like football's been taken off the air.
A little affection they might then show
*Then you think to yourself . . . here we go!*

***Michelle Donnelly (14)***
***The Wakeman School***

## BOYS

Boys - they think they're the best!
A cut above all the rest.
But you and I both know
It's all a lot of show.
Most of them think they rule
So now tell me who's the fool.
Some of them are okay, believe it, I know!
But what I generally think of boys
Is . . . *Oh no!*

***Jessica Allan (11)***
***The Wakeman School***

## Widow

The candle flickers with my every breath
Dancing figures on the wall.
Elegant and graceful.
The red embers remaining from the fire
Glow softly in the shadows.
A draught sends shivers through my spine
As I sit, sifting through my . . .
Our memories.

It is a cushion now, that hugs my chest
As I contemplate the silence.
The rip in the black linen offers no light
From the window.
The misty smell still lingers - strange
Compared with the scent of pot pourri.
Distant whining haunts the room - just
The wind . . . not a warning.

The initials *RB* shimmer on his box
His silver box that lit the cigars which
Could have, would have, killed him.
Ironic, placed next to the ribbon and cross
Within the leather box . . .
The day I knew was the day I grew old
Compensation does not exist in these cases
When he gave his life . . . he gave mine.

*His glory - my pain.*

***Patricia Clowes***
***The Wakeman School***

## GIRLS

Girls are always talking on the phone
I pity those poor boys they can't leave alone.
They flick through pages of magazines
big blond hunks are in their dreams.
They listen to 911, Five and the Backstreet boys.
They are too grown up-to play with toys.
Mascara, eyeshadow, blusher and red lipstick.
In high heels *click, click, click* they never stop.
Every Saturday she goes shopping in and out of shops - never stopping.
Every morning she brushes her hair
I'm the boy who will mess it up for a dare.
You can tell when they fancy a boy
Teasing, kicking, punching.
Oh! I wish they'd fancy me
*then I'd be full of glee!*

***Adam Brown (11)***
***The Wakeman School***

## MY BIG BROTHER

Ricky is my big brother.
He's really not like any other.
He can be mean to people
He can be mean to me
But he's really clever - you see!

Although he hides it well
So well, that no one can tell.
I'm really proud to be his
Little brother.
Because there is no-one other
*than Ricky . . .*

***Mark Chatwin (11)***
***The Wakeman School***

## Boys And Girls

Going up town, having fun
staying in the sun.
They go into a cake shop and buy a bun
don't offer you one
because they're shy . . .

Liking them, hating them.
Fancying them, dumping them.
What's the difference?

They're always keeping secrets.
Never telling anyone.
Can't go anywhere without make-up
or brushing their hair.

Dumping girls is fun
because you can get a better one!
Fussing about their hair . . .
*Never fair!*

***Steven Hill (11)***
***The Wakeman School***

## Boys

Sitting on the couch like a slob
Popcorn being stuffed into his gob.
'Coming out tonight?' I ask with a grin
'No, I might miss United win!'

Gels the hair as if it's a pet
I wonder if it's a girl he's met.
Slaps on a ton of aftershave to meet the crowd.
They mess about laughing and are extremely loud . . .

***Sallyanne Tuffin (11)***
***The Wakeman School***

## Gone Too Far!

This time mankind has gone too far.
Where the forest was, there's a Burger Bar.
The world's turning into a real mess
Shops are open twenty four hours.
They don't get any rest.
The world is covered with high-rise flats
Computers do all the work.
Now the workers are being sacked
But in the year 2000
Flowers break through the paving.
Mother Nature - the earth she's saving
The techno world . . . is no more!

***Kayley Hooker (11)***
***The Wakeman School***

## 2000

In three quarters of the world in the year 2000.
Celebrations, music and dancing.
But lonely in the other quarter.
Famine, poverty and death.
So there's laughter and fun for people
Do they think about people, lonely and miserable?
That's up to them . . .
Just think in 2000 about the people not celebrating
When the fireworks go bang . . . their lights go out.

***Sally Boucher (11)***
***The Wakeman School***

## MILLENNIUM

On December 31st 1999 I'll be at home
having a great party and thinking
about the Millennium Dome.

With midnight creeping on
the celebrations will start.
There will be all sorts of food
cake, sausages and a jam tart.

In the year 2000 - 13 I will be
So in the year 2000
*come and dance with me . . .*

***Lauren Adams (11)***
***The Wakeman School***

## BOYS ON GIRLS . . .

Girls keep secrets
never telling boys.
Can never be without make-up
but never need boys.
Dumping them's a pleasure
Specially at a party
Because you can find better.

Always telling Mummy if anything's wrong
never telling Daddy!
Never happy . . . always naggy.

***Stuart John James Halbert (11)***
***The Wakeman School***

## Boys

Boys are very annoying
they never do what you say.
They get dressed up for girls
and they wear loads of aftershave.

Boys think they're funny
and the best at playing football.
They think they are good at everything
really at nothing.

They are very lazy
glued to the TV
Bad-tempered and stupid
that's all they really need.

Sometimes they are best friends.
Sometimes they are enemies.
Sometimes they are sweet and nice
But most of the time . . . they are horrible!

***Lucy Phillips (12)***
***The Wakeman School***

## Colour

C olour all around us
O h! What stunning shades
L ingering for my eyes
O rangy, bluey, greys
U nusually bright and vivid
R evolting dull and horrid.

***Charlie Jones (12)***
***The Wakeman School***

## WILL IT BE . . .

It strikes midnight!
Start of the millennium year.
You can hear the singing
it's the *Auld Lang Syne.*

People dancing to pop music.
Oh, what a sight!
That from the stroke of midnight
was the first few hours of year 2000.

It's a new TV
bigger and better than the rest.
Money free from benefits,
So a life of leisure for everyone.

Bigger houses
and better computers.
Better people!
Will that be the future world?

Or will there be wars?
And gigantic roars.
Will they set animals free
that would be all my glee!

***Marc Beeston (11)***
***The Wakeman School***

## MIDNIGHT

Waiting, waiting another six minutes
Another six minutes till the New Year.
Waiting, waiting another five minutes
Waiting is boring but it's nearly here!
Waiting, waiting another four minutes.
I'm waiting very patiently - *but come on New Year.*
Waiting, waiting another three minutes,
My mum shouts at my brother 'Come here dear!'
Waiting, waiting another two minutes.
My mum is going to cry a great big tear.
Waiting, waiting another minute
The countdown is all that I can hear.
Waiting, waiting - *no more minutes.*
*Finally, the New Year is eventually here!*
A flash in the sky . . . a New Year has gone by.

***Alison Hughes (11)***
***The Wakeman School***

## THE TRUTH BEHIND GIRLS

Girls, always hiding secrets, always telling lies.
Always spending money
But never on the boys.
Always using make-up, always brushing their hair.
Never out of fashion even with their bags
The one thing that puzzles me is why use nail varnish?
Why do they love animals and not boys?
What is it about girlie talk that makes them gossip for hours!
The best thing about girls is that you can dump them
And even make them *cry!*

***Wesley Howes (12)***
***The Wakeman School***

## THE BOY THAT BURST

This is a tale of what a boy ate
one Friday night when it was late.
He started with some cherry drops
and then he moved to lolly pops.

Then he started on the toffee,
and cakes and fudge and cups of coffee.
Marshmallows and Black Jacks
and green and white Tic Tacs.
Chocolate Buttons, Pick-a-mix
wobbly jelly and Sherbet Dips.

He grew so fat, he grew so wide
that in the end . . . he burst and died.

***Laura Curran (13)***
***The Wakeman School***

## GIRLS ON BOYS

Boys from a girl's point of view
can be good, can be bad.
Some say they're good
some say they're bad.

How can they be bad?
When they help you mend your bike.
Get you out of trouble and all that
but I still say they're good and bad.

What do you think? Good or bad!
I've got it . . . *both!*
But they can't help it
They're . . . *boys!*

***Hayley Woodall (12)***
***The Wakeman School***

## ROLLER-COASTER

*Beep! Beep! Beep!*

We're off!
Slowly starting
Up we go
Getting higher
As we go . . .

At the top, we stop
For seconds we're there.
Putting our hands in the air.
Then we tilt and away
We go . . . go, go
Round, round, round and down
Up down round and round.

Then we drop in mid-air
Hoping the cart won't tear.
Slowly stopping to catch our breath
Then we go round . . . round again.

***Claire Smout (13)***
***The Wakeman School***

## THE GREAT WAR

And through the green mist they came,
Shouting, running for their piece of hard fought glory.
No medals greeted their open arms, only bullets,
Their only applause, the rattle of the machine guns.
They fall down, a look of horror in their clouded eyes,
disgust on their cracked and flaking grey faces.
The guns then find their booming voices,
Deafening ears, that listen for frightened minds.

***Jake Harvey (15)***
***The Wakeman School***

## The World

What will the planet be like in the future?
Hypnotic, in a trance or maybe Heaven.
What will it look like in the future?
Shattering, millions of colours or just a collage of light.

Will it be there in the future?
Haunted or taken over by aliens!
Will it move in the future?
Higher, lower or in the same place?

What will the people be like?
In a trance, or even robots!
What will the world be like in the future?
Perhaps the same as it is now.

***Victoria Musson (12)***
***The Wakeman School***

## Monsters

Monster, monster where are you hiding?
For I can smell that terrible breath.
Flap your wings, for that skilled gliding
I'm forty feet away, for which I'm near death.

Ergh! Those oozing feet
With those, you might even have poisoned the meat.
Ergh! That snotty nose,
Are you sure that's not in my garden hose.

Don't even think of stealing my soul.
Even though you're not as bad as the voodoo doll!

***David Wilson (12)***
***The Wakeman School***

## The Ride

Clank, clunk, churn and grind.
Fear, anticipation growing in my mind.
Metal on metal, oil burning oil.
Tension winding like a rusty old coil.
Pull, straining to reach the peak.
Mouth so dry, too afraid to speak
To the top . . .
*Stop!*
Plummeting, falling, helpless fear.
Thundering, screaming, earth coming near.
Faster, faster - to the drop.
Praying to God that my heart doesn't stop.
Twisting, turning, rushing lower and lower.
At last the turns become slower and slower.
Relief now pumping through my bones
Brake yanked on, reluctantly moans.
Stomach butterflies now dart away,
On solid earth I hope to stay.
A jerk, my safety belt takes the strain
*Oh no! My God! Here we go again . . .*

***Emma Johnson (12)***
***The Wakeman School***

## The Ride Of Fear!

Round and round
and up and down.
Back and forwards
from the ground.
Twisting, turning in the air.
Doing circles, makes you scared.

***Terrieann Williams (12)***
***The Wakeman School***

## ROLLER-COASTER

Steel clashing clanging on steel
the sounds of screaming screeches near.
Nearer and nearer they grow
the roller-coaster stops, stops . . .
Time to get on, butterflies in
my stomach.
The safety barrier clicks in
*Here we go o o o o!*
Climbing, climbing to the top.
We reach the peak and then we stop.
From the top, down, down we go.
Further and further, no one knows
when their
stomach will return.
When their eyes will open.
A curve in the line, a click just in
time.
A swirl in the dark, a pounding of the
heart.
A movement so fast, my ears blast.
A jerk forward, we come to a stop,
a stop
A stop at last, time to get off.
A minute away . . . I'll return another day!

***Dan Perry (12)***
***The Wakeman School***

## SEASIDE

Waves bash
and boats crash.
Seaweed's jumbled.
Seaweed's crumbled.
Lying under the sea.

Rock pools
big
rock pools
small
says my uncle Paul.
And look over there
says my little sis Claire.
A dolphin just came up
as just before
to see the shore
beautiful as it was before.

***Rebecca Martin (13)***
***The Wakeman School***

## WEATHER

W ind, wild as wild can be.
E ast it blows as gentle as can be.
A mazing sun now, here we go.
T ornadoes starting up in the snow.
H ail coming down as fast as can be .
E ast it blows, gentle to and fro
R ight now we have got more snow.
It's here again, Oh no!

***Ashley Lewis (12)***
***The Wakeman School***

## A World With No Future

Our world has no future
With pollution in the air
The streams are full of rubbish
Every flower is almost rare.

Our animals are endangered
The tiger, the rhino, the fox
Slaughtering, hunting, cubbing
The panda, the bear and the ox.

The bushes are losing condition
The leaves on the trees are dead
We need to take more care of our world
So keep that in your head.

***Jenny Bright (12)***
***The Wakeman School***

## Roller-Coaster

We're on the roller-coaster
We're going up the hill
Nearly at the top
We're going to get a thrill.

It's slowing down
It's now at the top
I'm very, very nervous
Now we start to drop.

Now were going upside down
I don't feel well
We're slowing down now
Well that's just swell.

***Thomas Knight (13)***
***The Wakeman School***

## First Love
## Last Love

Me and Kev fancied each other,
We fancied each other like mad.
He thought that I was the best girl,
I thought he was the best lad.

We used to go to the park together,
Or play on our bikes up the lane
After a month we kissed each other.
It was nice, so we did it again.

After a while Kev went strange.
He wouldn't come out to play.
I thought for a bit, then asked him why
He said 'cause he fancied Fay.

I cried and cried all through the night
I would've stopped if I could
After the tears I finally resolved
I'd finished with boys for good.

***Gina Cottey (12)***
***The Wakeman School***

## Urban March

I walk through blackened, tomb-like alleys,
Shoulders hunched, coat zipped up tight.
The shadow of doubt is not restricted to one valley
The primeval shadows cultivating fright.

Travelling through this apocalyptic nightmare
I see two ladies of the night fight, cat-like,
Kicking, gouging, tearing out hair,
I keep away, and take the next right.

Maimed, mutilated, shot in the head,
I guess the cops haven't got here yet
Yet another blameless man lies here dead.
A nearby junkie sighs, and sucks another pill in.

Here an electronics store, inside it's black,
Televisions still spewing out news
More murders, rapes, and dealings in crack,
Now an acclaimed expert, giving us his views.

Policemen sit in a warm interior,
Idle, insensitive, impotent too
Looking at me like I'm inferior
I shrug and think . . . *to hell with you!*

A noise behind, but now it's too late
A heavy blow to my head, no time to cry
Only ten yards from the police station gate.
And as I fall, I think: *What a stupid way to die!*

***Paul Thompson (13)***
***Thomas Telford School***

## SAVE, SAVE, SAVE THE DOLPHINS

The dolphins' glossy, grey, gorgeous skins shine,
Skimming and gliding through the ocean.
Talking in a *click, click, click, click . . .*
*Like small children just wanting to play.*

Save, save, save the dolphins!

As I sail the ferocious sea,
The friendly group appears.
Dancing and playing in front of the bow,
Having fun it seems.

Save, save, save the dolphins!

When the fishermen come, ready to kill,
The group decides to play.
But the nets come down, trapping them,
Dolphins twisting and turning trying to escape.

Save, save, save the dolphins!

'Those wretched dolphins are scaring our catch,' is the angry fishermen's cry.
One reaching for a gun watches as they play and squeal.
*Bang!* Trigger pulled. It hits its target - a young dolphin,
The school crowding around, confused, swims off.
The young one is dead!

Save, save, save the dolphins!

As the snail-slow boat chugs away,
The pup sinks slowly, disappearing.
'One less to worry about,' so they say.
But is that true?

Save, save, save the dolphins!

All have the right to live, dolphins, too.
Living side by side with each other.
No one creature should be killed because they get in the way . . .
This is what I say!

Save, save, save the dolphins!

***Hannah Bennett (11)***
***Thomas Telford School***

## Sunset

The light is dimming in the park,
Faded memories of long ago
An empty building as it goes dark
Nothing's like we used to know

A light that's dwindling all around
A little time to think of the past
A picture on the mantelpiece
That shows how much has changed

An old man sitting by the fire
He knows that day is nearly over
A woman sitting on a bench
To watch the sun as it goes down

A desolate street an empty town
It seems as if there's no one around
For some a final curtain call
A sun descending on the world

***James Stephan (13)***
***Thomas Telford School***

## NIGHTFALL

Today: Wind howled like a desperate child;
Winter arrived as soft as thunder;
One vulnerable sky - an endless shower,
Cruel to me as I've seen many better days.

This afternoon saw stars battling to make their appearance.
I begged the night to come quickly, damning long and
lengthy sunsets which see fatigue grasping his hunger.

I guess my bedtime long has passed,
those still conscious not as bothered with the time as I.
Still being juvenile, their night is young.
Members of their generation acting as torches through
the night giving them light until morning.

***Amy Clarke (14)***
***Thomas Telford School***

## DAWN

The sun rises above the trees
And the sound of cries is heard.
The large round sphere
Brings light to a life

That has never before been seen.
Its glow, gleaming gently as
It starts to grow, is now
Where all attention is given.

This glow keeps growing and
Becomes more intense,
And so the sky stretches, ready
For the long-awaited son.

***Joanna Clark (13)***
***Thomas Telford School***

## Drugs!

Drugs are evil,
Drugs are *bad!*
Drugs don't help,
They make you mad!

Why risk your life?
On something bad.
Look ahead,
Just don't be sad.

Just ask for help,
Don't be so shy.
Don't take drugs,
You might even *die!*

Drugs are evil,
Drugs are *bad!*
Drugs don't help,
They make you mad.

***Laura Padmore (1)***
***Thomas Telford School***

## A Witch

A witch is black,
She is the winter, cold,
In a chimney,
She is rainy,
She is a black hat and cape,
She is a dark chair,
She is bewitched,
She is a magic potion.

***Michael Ross (12)***
***Thomas Telford School***

## My Gran

I didn't really know her,
I first saw her when I was three,
Five years later she moved into an old people's home,
There was talk of her being sick,
A stroke is what she had,
But I didn't know what one of those was.

My mum and dad took me down to
Croydon to take me to my friend's.
They left me at his house and I wondered where they went.
They came back to say that my gran was better
So we could go back home.

Three weeks later we received a phone call,
It was from the old people's home,
My gran had another stroke,
Which was even worse,
So my dad went back to Croydon.

People dressed in black and brown,
The sun was shining bright,
As the brown, cold box came down the aisle,
Monsoons had hit people's eyes,
As people silently said their sorrow.

***Jason Harvey (14)***
***Thomas Telford School***

## Younger Brothers!

Younger brothers,
Obviously acceptable whilst babies,
Unfortunately they grow older, becoming
Nuisances!
Grabbing my things,
Eating my sweets,
Rabbiting on about nothing.

Boring my friends with football tales and
Revealing my secrets.
Opening my mail,
Tampering with my CD's
Honestly, *this has to stop!*
Eventually they understand, as
Revenge is sweet, unlike
Sister in a *temper!*

***Amy Jones (12)***
***Thomas Telford School***

## I Really Hate . . .

I really hate a lot of things,
most I do despise.
But most of all I really hate,
people telling lies.

Spiders make me shiver,
when they scutter all about.
Whenever I see one,
I always scream or shout.
They run around the living room,
on the kitchen floor,
they run along desk tops and under every door.

Another thing I really hate,
is arguments with my brother.
But being really truthful.
I wouldn't swap him for another.

*I hate . . .*

***Kerry Foreman (11)***
***Thomas Telford School***

## Sundown

When the sun goes down in the sleepy fishing town,
The tide comes up to meet the beach,
With fingers that stretch and reach.

The sun creeps down the cloudless sky,
No longer does it hang up high.
The breeze from off the sea is fresh,
It's soothing touch to cool your flesh.

The sun slides down the soft peach sky,
It's disappearing from my eye.
The sea is tinted orange and pink,
Into which the sun does sink.

It's gone from view,
It's melted down.
No longer lighting this fishing town.

***Ashley M Burd (13)***
***Thomas Telford School***

## An Emotional Poem

The world turns,
The sand falls,
And blood runs cold.
Nothing lasts; nothing endures.
All is crushed,
And ground to dust beneath the wheels of time.
Warriors, kings - kingdoms,
Where time is the master we all are victims.
The only question is, who will be the first,
And who will be the last.

***Neil Evans (13)***
***Thomas Telford School***

## Slave From The Kitchen

As I gaze out of the window
On to the beach of the past,
The tide has washed my life away
And the sun has set, at last.

My young life almost over
But nothing has been done,
I'm the slave from the kitchen
The one they just call Mum.

The seasons slowly passing
But no one else can see
The wasted time so precious
Passing right in front of me.

***Laura Pitchford (13)***
***Thomas Telford School***

## My Emotional Poem

He was put on this earth as a loving friend
Sent by God as an angel
He would listen to my problems
And would give me love back.

Every day he was there as himself or the angel
Scurrying around in his own little world.
50cm by 30cm was all he would have
But it felt like an acre to him.

He was a lovely hamster with his appealing face
But he had to go back to God
Like a video you hire from a shop
But he is always here in my heart to remember.

***Craig Johnson (14)***
***Thomas Telford School***

## EVERYTHING HAS TO DIE

On the 11th May.
It was a warm summer's day.
I came home to find
my mum crying.

To find out that my granddad
Was dead felt like a needle
piercing my head.
My sister started crying.

On our way to Leicester
We looked up at the
red sky, like a blanket of
blood it reminded me
everything has to die.

***Tim Baker (13)***
***Thomas Telford School***

## THE MACHINE

Lifeless limbs hangs limply as time passes by,
Stiff backed he waits endlessly for the order,
An empty can, eyes full of sadness
With no soul, but a heart that weeps
Oily tears for what could have been.

A simple little diversion when life had just begun,
Just one turn in another direction,
To be the driver of someone's joy,
A Christmas gift, a child's present
Chosen and cheerfully, chuffing along the line.

A dream rudely interrupted, reality occurs
A button pressed, a sudden burst of power,
A shocking surge of suction rouses
The vessel from its reverie, then
A roar of protest before the sweetest hum.

What terror is unleashed, as all is devoured
Only the *monster* is safe from the demon's
Sucking and swallowing, spiders whole
Bodies disappear with a scream
Or is it just the creature searching for his dream.

***Ruth Broughton (13)***
***Thomas Telford School***

## Hot Or Cold

The rain descends spitting on the window,
Pouring down and down for an hour or so.
As earth spins and the sun hides behind the clouds,
Like a child winning a game, so happy, so proud.

And this thing that sits in the corner alone,
Glowing like a baby that has crawled on its own.
Fills the air with warmth and gives you such pleasure,
Only you'll take it for granted forever and ever.

You know what it does. You know how it works.
Yet you use it only for one thing, how does it feel, is it hurt?
If it breaks you replace it as easy as that,
You'll buy something better more expensive more VAT.

And now it does break but what can it do,
As it watches it's replacement shining and new,
So this thing that sits in the corner alone,
Crying like a baby that has failed on its own.

***Alex Reynolds (13)***
***Thomas Telford School***

## If Only . . .

Another boring Monday morning
Same old dull routine
As I work I often wonder
How life might have been.

I cook and clean and wash and wipe,
Put the dinner on the table
Instead I could be a career woman
But now I'm just not able.

I should have stayed on at my school
To pass all my exams
Instead I left when I was 16
'Cause I had other plans.

All I thought of was the money
I was so eager to earn
But what sort of job would I get
When I didn't stay on and learn?

I could have been a lawyer,
A doctor or a vet
Instead of a housewife and mother
With far too much regret.

So back to the old routine
Opportunities all gone
I can't turn back the clock now
There's more housework to be done!

***Hayley Carter (14)***
***Thomas Telford School***

## DEATH

It was a cold winters day in New York
I will remember that day forever.
Because it was the day our family changed
I will remember that day forever.

We had told him not to go into the
gangster area. We told him it was dangerous,
would he listen, no.
He went in headstrong and arrogant.

He was only there for a few minutes because
as he walked he was mown down by
a hail of gun fire.
I ran to him ignoring the bullets but I was too late.

He was dead. My parents couldn't handle it,
they were depressed and sad. I tried
to be strong, it just didn't work. When they got home
from work they just went up to their room and cried.

At the day of the funeral it was a sombre
mood. Even his mates who were normally rowdy
were sat with their heads in their hands.
It had just sunk in I had lost my brother.

*I will remember that day forever.*

***David Cheetham (14)***
***Thomas Telford School***

## PET SHOP

Snoozing, snuffling, sniffing, sucking,
listening to the squawk of the birds.
Four brown puppies in a pet shop
Dream together.

Grunting, gumming, grappling, growling,
listening to the patter of the hail outside.
Four brown puppies in a pet shop
Wake together.

Jumping, joining in, joyful, juvenile,
listening to the bang of the door.
Four Brown puppies in a pet shop
Play together.

Licking, lapping, lunching, lustfully,
listening to the crack of the dog food tin.
Four brown puppies in a pet shop
Eat together.

Twitching, turning, tossing, touching,
listening to the gentle drip of the broken tap.
Four brown puppies in a pet shop
Sleep together.

***Amanda Lomas (11)***
***Thomas Telford School***

## Sunset Times

The day ends,
The sun sets,
A brilliant flame of light,
People watch and think, well
Tomorrow's another day.

People cry,
We wonder why,
But then everyone has to die.

Another day ends,
Clouded over by the shadow
Of Obscurity,
It has been a long day.

A granddad
An OAP
A death no one cared to see.

Once again the sun sets,
And everyone is shocked,
Ended by a violent storm,
What a way for a day to end.

The police continue investigations,
The newsperson said,
For today a man was found murdered,
An angry blow to the head.

So once again a life's sun sets,
And in truth we wonder at it,
Another end,
Another loss,
Another sunset time.

***Daniel Koczy (13)***
***Thomas Telford School***

## WHY IS THERE RACISM?

This is not fair this is not right,
Let other people into our sight.

If you think about this situation,
Does yellow like purple?
Does green like blue?
Do blacks like white?
It's really up to you.

This is not fair this is not right,
Let different cultures into our sight.

This world is a big wide place,
Does is really matter what colour the face?
Each individual person has their own belief,
At the end of the day we may all be wrong,
So what, is it fun to give others grief?

This is not fair, this is not right,
Let other beliefs into our sight.

God has not made our world to be bad,
Or to be cruel to one another,
If we leave this problem for many more years
There's certainly going to be more than tears.

This is not fair, this is not right,
Let others' points of view into our sights.

Different people do think different things,
There's nothing wrong with this
Why can't people put their thoughts across
Without being in danger for doing so.

This is not fair, this is not right,
Let other people's pride or misfortune release into our sights.

Do we think about others in this world,
Do we let different people have their fair say,
People fighting in wars, to their God they do pray,
All they want is to make peace, this very day,
Why can't people accept this,
No one likes being treated bad,
We are all equal.

Let's put our thoughts together and change this style of life.

***Elizabeth Inwood (11)***
***Thomas Telford School***

## A Fire Station

A fire station is full of movement,
Ringing bells all the time.
Sirens wailing,
Water cascading,
All in this one place.

Shouting and bawling,
Fire engines roaring,
Ladders creaking and old.
Loud and exciting,
Lots of fire-fighting,
All in this one place.

Running and climbing,
Their speed is so blinding,
As they hurtle down the pole.
Telephone calling,
Even more bawling,
All in this one place.

***Max Pownall (11)***
***Thomas Telford School***

## The Wind

The wind is a raging lion
Roaring in the sky,
It runs around its endless cage
Up there very high.

It claws its way through the sky
It tears the clouds apart,
It pierces the moon and the sun,
Fiercely like a dart.

The wind blows on towards a hilltop
And engulfs it all in one,
It then moves on towards a mountain
It comes but then has gone.

The wind is a raging lion
Roaring in the sky,
It runs around its endless cage
Up there very high.

***David Westwood (11)***
***Thomas Telford School***

## Mysterious Creature

It appeared in the sky like a crescent moon,
A silvery vision brightening up the gloom.
Just a smiling mouth and two rows of teeth,
No flesh above, no flesh beneath.

The two bright coals of gleaming eyes,
Were next to pierce the dark blue skies.
They smouldered with mystery and were full of knowing
As they watched intently, still brightly glowing.

Just when it seemed to have no substance,
A further more ghostly yet earthly occurrence.
Prints of paws appeared upon the ground,
Yet still there came not the slightest of sounds.

I closed my eyes, it must be a dream,
Things were even stranger than they seemed,
But when I opened them again to stare,
Disappearing slowly into the midnight air . . .

*The outline of the elusive Cheshire cat!*

***Chloë Whittle (12)***
***Wrekin College***

## The Nocturnal Mystery

I've heard of a
Monster that comes
Out at night.
He's covered in prickles,
A most awesome sight.
He doesn't croak as
I had expected
But lets out a squeak
As though being dissected.
He dines on beetles,
Snails and slugs
And I'm told he'll
Eat a variety of bugs.
When approached he
Curls up into a ball
And he hides away
From the start of the fall.

***Edward Eaton (12)***
***Wrekin College***

## Months Of The Year

Every year you get the months,
They're something you can't change,
February destroys the pattern
That seems very strange.
January is the first,
The start of our new year.
February, the shortest month,
With all the winter's fear.
March is the wind bringer,
And the start of spring.
April showers will come, so they say,
But they don't and it's May.
By May all the snow has disappeared,
Sheep are preparing to be sheared.
Flowers are in full bloom: It must be June,
Lovely sunny sun and crisp white moon.
By July the summer is here,
Jumping animals like the deer.
August and summer is at its peak,
The sun is anything but meek.
September and here comes the fall,
Trees are bare, thin and tall.
October and autumn's in full swing,
Outside I can hear church bells ring.
November and winter starts to creep,
Around the corner into our world.
December and snow starts to fall,
With my cup of cocoa I have curled.

That's all the months from beginning to end.
We start again to try and make amends.

***Harriet Tierney (12)***
***Wrekin College***

## SEASONS

Autumn's here, conkers glisten and glow,
Fall down for our personal show
Dropping down onto a blanket,
Of fallen, spreading leaves.
Flowers wither, lose their petals,
Everything starts to die.

Winter comes, the cold sets in,
Old dead leaves go in the bin.
Crops are gathered in by farmers,
Safe for the months to come.
Snow falls, snowmen built,
Dressed up in warm, snug clothes.

Spring arrives, the new life comes,
Lambs, calves, to name but some.
The hibernating animals return,
As the cold drifts away.
The sun starts to shine an orangy-glow.
Just to show new start in life.

Summer's here, finally come,
Very good news for some.
Sun breaking through the clouds
Glowing its fiery glow.
Giving red skies at night,
Showing us the heat to come.

***Sarah Frost (12)***
***Wrekin College***

## Frustrating Time

One minute it's there,
The next it's not,
There is never too much,
But always not enough.
You're either early or late,
But never on time,
As the seconds tick . . .
Tick right away.
Seconds, minutes, hours, days,
Disappearing like sand through your fingers.
Waiting, waiting,
For your moment to come . . .
*Death*

***Nicol Mason (12)***
***Wrekin College***

## The Dark

The wood is as still as death,
And as quiet as a graveyard,
Everything is listening to silence,
Even silence listening to silence.

The world is lost
Lost in darkness,
No one there to help you,
Nothing but the dead.

The darkness is as black as coal
And as thick as mud,
The only light which shines through
Is that of the small moon behind the trees.

***Sam Marnham (11)***
***Wrekin College***

## TIME

*Tick tock goes the clock*
On the sitting room wall
Red, yellow colours bright
Like the sun's shining light.

Days, months, years go by
How time really flies
Several minutes, several hours
Is time really ours?

Winter's almost over
Summer's on its way
Autumn's coming soon now
So there's no time for delay.

Travelling in an aeroplane
Time just really flies
I can even get there
Before your very eyes.

Sometimes time goes slowly
Seconds into minutes
Days turn into centuries
Minutes into hours.

Clockwise hands turn around
Slowly sometimes, other quick
Round and round on the face
All year round it goes.

***Helen Bailey (12)***
***Wrekin College***

## I Love Sport

This is a list of my best sports,
Skating always steals my thoughts,
You didge, you dodge,
And skate around
Believe it or not it's just three pounds

Another sport which I think rules
Has got to be basketball it's so cool
Dribbling, shooting
Just says it all,
But you can't play it without a ball.

The third sport which I desire
Is rugby a game to inspire,
You run about with the ball,
You pass, kick, tackle
And always fall.

The fourth sport has got to be cricket
Your aim is to hit the wicket,
You bowl with a cricket ball
The batsman hits and then he calls,
And runs around the small sticks which look like twiglets

But last of all is of course football
Which you play with a ball,
And when you score you always shout, 'Goal.'
This sport really is the best
And towers over all the rest.

***Luke Townsend (12)***
***Wrekin College***

## My Cat

Ollie is my cat
He's black, white and fat.
Ollie is sweet, he is a male
And he has a very cute tail.

I love Ollie, he loves me,
I like the way be eats his tea.
At night he always sleeps on my bed,
'Goodnight Ollie, sweet dreams,' I said.

Ollie is plump and very heavy,
And he really has a big belly.
He sleeps all day in the sun,
'Do you enjoy your life? Is it fun?'

Ollie is twelve, an old cat.
But still he can catch mice and rats
His sweet face looks as though he's smiling,
I understand him, when he's crying.

10 long years I've been with Ollie
When I was little he was my dolly
He really is clever,
And he's mine forever.

I talk to him of what I did,
He seems to understand 'cause he always cries back
He is the best on the earth
From the very day of his birth.

When Ollie is in a bath, cleaning,
It looks as though he's doing synchronised swimming.
I want to stay with him wherever I go,
And I want him to follow me calling, 'Keiko, Keiko.'

***Keiko Tanaka (13)***
***Wrekin College***

## FOOTBALL

Football is a wonderful game
No other sport is quite the same.
My friends and I play more and more
Until at the end we find out the score.

On Wednesdays we have a footy match
Our keeper needs to learn how to catch!
The football pitch is quite small
Almost as small as the school hall.

The next week we're back to play
It is another footy day.
Football's always really fun
People play it, rain or sun.

I yell, I scream to get the ball
I let them know I'm there to call.
I get the ball, no time to rest
I shoot and then I'm the best.

*Wahey,* now we've won the game
I'll stop and now retire in fame.
Now I go home and think about
The other team scoring nowt.

***Tom Didonato (12)***
***Wrekin College***

## LONELINESS

In the cool weightless night air,
a child wanders,
the water glitters like sparkling diamonds,
the soft touch of the wet sand,
as the clouds drift across the transparent sky,
the boy watches intently,
as the waters roll onto the dark sand.

The child's eyes reflect the distant sea,
the single beam of light shone down from the heavens above
to the young child, it was as if God had spoken,
the child crouched and lifted,
once,
twice, then success.
The child made what looked like a giant crab,
the water splashed over the tiny limbs,
the white ran smoothly back from where it came,
then all was still,
the black clouds filled the sky.

***Charlotte Rogers (13)***
***Wrekin College***

## In Bed With Darkness

I can't get to sleep,
My feet are all hot
And the only light in my room
Is the outside spotlight peeping through
The curtains.

What's that tapping?
It must be the dog
But what if it's not?
It could be a thug,
Out to get me!

The dog's barking but what at?
I'm all hot now,
Silence is jumping out at me,
I can hear myself breathing
It's too intense!
The light must go on!

***Tom Burgess (11)***
***Wrekin College***

## TIME

When you have to wait
It seems like a waste of time
When there are millions of things
you could be doing
I find it both peaceful
But frustrating

There are lots of different clocks
For example, fun, whacky, coloured clocks
Or even cute little cuckoo clocks
And even huge wise grandfather clocks
In a way they are just like people
Every one is unique in its own special way

Time is like the grandfather of earth
It's been through everything
The past with the dinosaurs
The present right now
And the future,
Well it will be there when our children's
children are around

Everything revolves around time
Every second in life
You are a second closer to death
Every minute, every hour, every year
Your life just ticks away
Till suddenly it stops
Like your battery has run out
But not even the best doctors
can replace it
So take care of your battery
and enjoy your time.

***Yasmine Charafeddine (13)***
***Wrekin College***

## FLIGHT

The young girl
stared harshly
at war overhead.

The little girl's eyes
glazed up
and turned away
as the bright lights flashed at her.

She stood
clutching hard to her doll,
glaring at the sky,
waiting for the next plane
to come crashing down.

On the clear breezy day,
all could be seen well,
with glazes and the fires
gliding,
slowly,
softly
down.

Her brother was working,
paying no attention
to the firelit sky.
If he could,
he would be up there
fighting (like a soldier).

***Linda Goransson (13)***
***Wrekin College***

## The Orphanage

The bony fingers snatched
At the top of my arm,
As the long taloned blood-red painted fingernails
Clawed into my arm.
'Look child! Head up! Pick up your feet, child!'
My eyes drifted up and looked into the hard angular face
Then my eyes drifted back to the cobbled pavement.
We got there.
The big black door slowly creaked ajar
To reveal a young, motherly-looking girl.
My aunt's scratchy voice began to take flight
As I stared.
'Mother dead . . .'
She said.
'Father left . . .'
I wept
'No money . . .'
Who cares!
I was jabbed in the back, and left.
No kiss, no goodbyes
Just left
There,
Alone,
Afraid.
'Come with me, my darling'
Said a soft voice, a warm hand clasped mine.
'No need to be afraid, just sit tight'
I sit, glaring into my lap
My hands cling onto my dress sweating
Like tiny balls of transparent marbles
My hands cling on to my black dress, the same dress
I wore when my ma was carried out.
The sweat looks like the pearls around my aunt's neck.
'Look up, sweetie!'
What's going to happen to me?

I don't know
Unknowingly, I glanced up,
Looked up into the big, black evil eye.
*Click!*
I was captured for life,
On a still
Of my life,
Will it get better?
I was led away into a silent corridor
Click! Click! went the young nursemaid's shoes.
'Here is your bed
Take off your shoes
Be good, do you hear?'
I slipped off my old black shoes
And crawled into the itching bed
Looking at the plain, white ceiling
The gentle snores of the children next to me
The calmness encloses me
I drift off
Into the silence.

***Stephanie Pearce (13)***
***Wrekin College***

## FALLEN ANGEL

The boy fell after
The girl threw the stone.
From the top of the
Barracks to the sharp
Rocky bottom, he fell.

The evil girl with
Her eyes of fire
Ran into the distance
Over the sun-swept
dunes.

The boy at the
Bottom stuck on
A rock with a point
At the top that went
Through his heart.

He died whilst
His friend stood
And watched the
Blood pour from
His unwanted body.

***Chris Sheldon (14)***
***Wrekin College***

## HIPPO JUNGLE

The monstrous animals hunt for food,
Their huge ears and teeth shine by the moon,
The snapping noises they make at night,
They're always silent when it's light.

In the day they're nice and quiet,
They're calm and silent,
Gliding through the water playing with their friends,
The gentle giant kills the silence when the day ends.

They rip the guts and liver from their prey,
Then they just wait for the next day.
The fear in the eyes of the hippo
Looking out for a predator.

Thieving food off each other,
These crude huge monsters eat,
How they act is like a crazy mongrel,
And how they like it in 'hippo jungle'.

***Thomas Swann (12)***
***Wrekin College***

## The Little Girl Who Had To Try

As the girl looked up to the heavens,
She saw the most beautiful thing,
A wonderful array of colours,
So brilliant she nearly could sing.

Her brother said 'Down in the shelter!'
Her mother said, 'Hurry, quick, quick!'
Little girl stood there, thinking,
'She was always one to pick!'

Suddenly, a booming noise in the sky,
'Down in the shelter, or we'll all die!'
'Mummy, Mummy, where are we going?'
'Down to the shelter, to hide from a Boeing!'

Down into the dark, dank cellar, they went,
Trying to hide from the plane's descent.
Little girl stopped and started to cry,
'Carry on dear, we all have to try!'

The little girl is now an adult,
And often wonders why,
Her decrepit mother, and her handsome brother,
Had to die to make her try.

***James Stanton (14)***
***Wrekin College***

## Moonlight

Harsh, irate voices splinter the night;
glares scar deep summer serenity.
Colossal ships navigate silently into harbour,
secure after voyaging undulating oceans.

Another salty bead trickles off the tips of her lashes,
down over her flushed cheek.
Mild breezes skim over a silvery surface;
ripples catching the moonlight glisten invitingly.

Once, each would have died for the other;
now they stand stubbornly.
A lone seal observes from his sand dune,
glassy eyes reflecting urban lights.

With a resolute gesture she turns.
Sad cries drift across balmy air.
All he can do is mumble and look away in guilt.
Moist, velvety skin twitches as the seal dives.

Tired flippers score lines through fluctuating water
with gentle splashes.
A reunited group glides out of the safe harbour
into their vast, mysterious world.

***Helen Phillips (13)***
***Wrekin College***

## LOST IN THE WOOD

The leaves rustling,
The breeze blowing,
*Ouuuuooooh! Ouuuuooooh!*
What was that?
*Ouuuuooooh! Ouuuuooooh!*
Just my little brother trying to scare me.
'I'm frightened' he said,
So . . . so . . . am I,
*Ahhh!*
Something had grabbed me by the leg
What was it?
Where did it come from?
A light ahead of us faded, faded, faded.
Something was watching us,
I listened,
Every creature was listening with me,
Silence was listening to silence,
I ran towards the light,
It was a headlamp of a car,
Looked around,
It was no one,
We were as silent as a misty graveyard,
I jumped up,
What's happening?
Somebody,
Something was in front, in front of us,
I wasn't asleep with my brother anymore.
It's . . . it's a . . .
*Phew!*
It's only a mad dream,
Maybe . . .

***Edward Whittaker (11)***
***Wrekin College***

## Lost In Africa

Way down deep in the middle of the jungle,
I was lost for at least an hour,
And I was confused,
My feelings were unsure,
Didn't know where to turn,
No friends,
No help,
No way out!
Wishing I was home,
Depressed I was lost,
No civilisation,
Of mankind,
I'd never seen such loneliness,
Thirsty and hungry,
Hearing strange noises,
It feels like I am being watched
By someone,
By something,
Taking caution at every step,
The night getting colder,
I'm getting goose bumps all over my body.
The night is gone,
The day has risen.

***Guayarmina Perdomo-Molyneux (11)***
***Wrekin College***

## I Am Lost In The Jungle

I am lost in the jungle,

A ll alone.
M y friends are nowhere about.

L oads of monkeys are screaming,
O n an island without food.
S cared and confused,
T hirsty and alone.

I n complete panic I realise
N othing can be done.

T errified I start to run,
H elp is nowhere about.
E verybody has deserted me.

J ungles are unpleasant things,
U nknown places full of mysterious things.
N othing can destroy it but man,
G ot to have wood is what they say.
L eave it alone, some sensible people say,
E vermore we are destroying it.

***Rebecca Parker-Brittain (12)***
***Wrekin College***

## AFTER-SHOCK

Lost and alone
Anxious and afraid
I walk through the forest in the pouring rain
The heat in the morning
Beating all around
I'm thirsty and hungry and odd creatures abound.
Confused with the strangeness
Tormented, timid, petrified
Trapped in this mysterious world . . .
My face is wet with tears.
Will no one come to help?
Suddenly . . . a noise
As a helicopter sweeps over
I say to myself 'Could it be . . .
I'm going to be rescued?'
But no, it carries on going.
For a minute I had faith
But my hopes are now down
As I carry on walking amongst the menacing trees.

I begin to black out,
There is no hope;
Then suddenly, *darkness* . . .

***Thomas Bonigal (11)***
***Wrekin College***

## Lost

You're lost, alone, no one around and continually running.
Out there he is watching you . . .
Somewhere in the dense background.
You're thirsty and helpless,
Nowhere to go.
Scrambling up rocks.
He is there.
His eyes glinting in the moonlight,
Yet you can't tell what he is,
Animal, beast or human!
You're petrified, looking for civilisation,
But you're alone, no one, you're alone.
You hear a crack
Nervous as you are, you venture over.
It's a vole!
But *the thing* is still out there.
You're worried, cold and depressed.
This does not help the situation.
*The thing* takes a leap.
Growls but misses its prey.
You're running now
But this time it's after you.
You look around . . . it's a *black panther*.
It takes a leap.
Then everything goes quiet
Because your species is extinct.

***Ewan Caird (12)***
***Wrekin College***

## Lost

I am in the jungle,
Sleeping in a tree,
I dream of playing with monkeys.
I wake up,
Thinking of my dinner,
And I go up to a big tree,
And cut down some bananas.
Some monkeys come to me,
And I share the bananas,
But I haven't got a lot
So I cut down some coconuts
And eat them!

I was going to the sea,
It was very cold,
I caught a fish,
And a bear caught a fish for me.
So I cut down some coconuts
And I made coconut juice
For the bear.
I went back to my house,
But I couldn't sleep,
So I drank the water
But I could not sleep.

***Haruna Kimpara (11)***
***Wrekin College***

## BLACK VELVET

Silence as deep as death,
So peaceful, not frightening at all.
You're on your own but you're not scared,
Pitch velvet blackness cushioning around everything,
The only light was a single star.

You have a queer feeling,
You don't know what you just have,
It's starting to get creepy
It's not as special anymore.

You start hearing things,
You see shapes,
Now you can see a person,
Shut your eyes and they're gone.

It's quiet again, no noise at all,
I'm not scared anymore,
The tiredness is overwhelming.

I lay my head down,
Shut my eyes,
*I'm . . .*

***Katie Fellowes (12)***
***Wrekin College***

## The Horse

Standing lonely
In the corner
Like a bullied child
He longs for the wild.

The soft dark eyes
On his gentle face
Seem warm and comforting
In this cold dark place.

His muscles tense up
As he takes the strain,
With a challenging rear
He tears away from the chain.

Off into the night
And like a bird
He gallops and gallops
Until no more is heard.

A piercing whinny
Cuts through the night sky
He stops dead in his tracks
His head held up high.

Then out of the distance
They come into sight.
Three galloping horses
Two black and one white.

The horse, he stands watching
This magnificent three,
Then as a foursome together
They run to be *free.*

***Georgie Hodson (12)***
***Wrekin College***

## THE LAND ROVER

It was 7.00 on a cold wet morning.
We approached the dirty, smelly Land Rover.
I got in the passenger seat and slammed
the heavy door behind me.

My uncle turned the shiny key
and the engine revved up.
There was a smell of petrol burning
in the engine.
Smoke came pouring out of the exhaust.

Very slowly but surely
my uncle drove down to the rusty old gate.
I got out and opened it,
it squeaked very loudly.
We then moved on into the field
very slowly indeed.
We travelled to a wilderness
which looked like a jungle.

Slowly we moved into the wilderness,
first we drove through a ditch,
it felt as though I was on a trampoline.
We then wended around trees,
through valleys and lots of other obstacles.

We then returned. We drove out of
the wilderness and back into the
muddy field.

We returned to the rusty gate and
parked it up, back in its position.

***Ben Evans (13)***
***Wrekin College***

## THE WOLF

High on a cliff stands
A hunchback beast
Black fur like silk,
Glaring eyes,
Claws like knives,
His mouth drools as he looks for his prey.

It's dark and shadowed on this fearful night.

The silence like fear
As he pricks up his ears
The scuffling of webbed feet
A minuscule creature is seen
The wolf freezes and suddenly pounces
The snap of his jaws
The flesh is ripped and torn

He prowls back to the pack with his prey
To feed his young
This creature is eaten just like that!
The young are now asleep
Quiet and peaceful
The wolf not deadly,
But just feeding his young
*The wolf we don't know!*

***Rebecca Crump (12)***
***Wrekin College***

## LOST

Deep in the jungle where the monkeys sing
There was a little child, very little indeed.

Deep in the jungle where the lions roar
The helpless and timid boy felt cold and hungry.

Deep in the jungle where the hippos wail
The little boy frightened and upset.

Deep in the jungle where the snakes slither,
The child is hot and thirsty.

I am that boy, so nervous and confused,
Helpless and lonely and miles from home.

***James Boden (11)***
***Wrekin College***